CHASING THE DARK

*Fly fishing and bird hunting through
early mornings and late nights*

JOSEPH JACKSON

KENMORE, WA

Alaska Book Adventures™

6524 NE 181st St., Suite 2, Kenmore, WA 98028

Epicenter Press is a regional press publishing nonfiction books about the arts, history, environment, and diverse cultures and lifestyles of Alaska and the Pacific Northwest. For more information, visit www.EpicenterPress.com

Chasing the Dark
Copyright © 2024 by Joseph Jackson

All rights reserved. No part of this publication may be reproduced, stored in a retrieval system, or transmitted in any form by any means, electronic, mechanical, photocopying, recording, or otherwise, without the prior written permission of the publisher. Permission is given for brief excerpts to be published with book reviews in newspaper, magazines, newsletters, catalogs, and online publications.

Cover design: Scott Book
Interior design: Melissa Vail Coffman

Library of Congress Control Number: 2024935008

ISBN: 978-1-684922-18-5 (Trade Paperback)
ISBN: 978-1-684922-19-2 (Ebook)

For my Oncorhynchus, my Cordelia, my Cora
—I hope you like the dark too, little one

INTRODUCTION: EARLY MORNINGS I'VE KNOWN

I'M BARRELING THROUGH DARKNESS AS BLACK AS a raven's wing, oriented only by the faraway rind of a moon and the clasping reach of my headlights. There's coffee in the thermos and a rimfire rifle in the backseat. I want to be there before sunrise.

Today's mission takes place in Alaskan November, though it could just as easily have taken place in June or September when the rimfire would've been a fly rod. The real major difference is the hour. In August, I have to leave the apartment at two in the morning to be where I want to be before dawn, but today, with the slow crawl of impending winter, I have to wait until seven to hit the road. No point in being there before you can see to shoot, and on a day like today you might as well let the sun show up if only to make it feel warmer. I've got all the time in the world, it seems—nowhere to be but tromping listlessly through the boreal in search of snowshoe hares—but with each passing mile the dawn moves in, and the darkness fades.

I had a friend in college who summed up this darkness quite neatly one spring day about six years ago. I'd stumbled into eight o'clock class after a night of burbot fishing, looking haggard and reeking of chopped lamprey. His face crawled over the cover of his textbook.

"Joe," he said, "it's light more than twenty hours a day, and yet you still choose to fish in the dark."

This was a time of year when he was right to question my methods: April. Alaska had rolled out of its wintery slumber, meaning that daylight, a commodity which in the far north can become as precious as gold or petroleum, was prevailing. The sun would come up at something like four in the morning, and it would bob across the horizon until midnight. Burbot fishing during its four-hour absence was both irrational and, considering college finals week was bearing down upon us, a bit reckless. But I had to.

Burbot, being a mostly nocturnal species, feed best in the dark. When the rivers are sealed beneath three feet of ice they don't tend to care so much, but during breakup season, timing matters. And it's not just for burbot; name an animal and chances are that it's more active in the dark than in the daylight, or at least in the transitional periods of dawn and dusk. Snowshoe hares, for example. Or steelhead. There are biological reasons for this, of course, but all we really have to know is that, if you're a serious outdoorsman, you should be in the woods or on the stream while this is going on. That's how I've come to operate. That's the only right way to do it.

IT'S HARD TO RECALL THE FIRST time I woke up before dawn—you know, the first time I snapped awake in the dark and pawed for a pair of socks because I had somewhere to *be* and something to *do*—but the best I can say is that it was an ice fishing excursion when I was seven or eight years old. Either way, it wasn't so much the anticipation of the experience that yanked me from dreams to consciousness; it was the thought of Dad having to wait on me.

This first expedition marked the start of an annual tradition: ice fishing in the western Rockies of Colorado with our family friend Jim Hill and whichever of his four daughters he could con into joining him. Usually we'd gear up and leave the afternoon of our last day of school before winter break. My brother, Hank, and I would stuff the truck full of puffy winter jackets and piles of wool socks because, even in our youthful idiocy, we knew there were few things colder than sitting in a folding chair on a bare, windswept lake.

Jim had some friends who lived out that way named Ted and Sue. Ted worked at a wood pellet factory and Sue ran the post office, and they had a cozy little home not far from the lakes we fished. Now that I think about it, I can't remember ever seeing Ted and Sue's place in the daylight.

We'd get there and unload whatever crap we brought (Hank and I would take several trips, dropping socks with each one), then we'd settle into the hammock of conversation that tends to build up when you haven't seen each other in a while. There'd be a football game on that no one would watch, and the sonic boom of Ted's laughter and the pattering of shuffling dogs would go well into the night. Be it several hours later or just a few, Ted would stuff his gigantic woodstove full and we'd all take that as the cue to head to bed. Hank and I would lay out sleeping bags, and it didn't matter if it was zero degrees outside or absurdly colder—we always felt like we were sleeping inside a brick oven.

I would awaken to the sounds of men's voices, long before the sun peaked out. Ted, Jim, and Dad were always the first ones awake, and they'd talk about the price of heating oil or the mallards they busted last fall in remarkably quiet undertones. Their fingers would be hooked through mugs of coffee, and, more often than not, Jim would be prodding at some bacon in a fry pan. It was here that I discovered that I absolutely loathed the feeling of other people being up before me, so I'd wriggle out of my sleeping bag and make it apparent to the men that I was awake. I wouldn't partake in their coffee, no chance—back then I hated the stuff—but I was *up,* alright. I couldn't really partake in their conversations, either, except by offering occasional grins and nods as if I knew what the hell they were talking about. But when it came time to blast the diesels to life and head off in pursuit of ice-bound trout, there was one thing you could bet on: They wouldn't be waiting on me.

Ice fishing was a simple affair as I gaze back on it, but at the time it seemed as indecipherable as demotic Egyptian. Ted, being the local who notoriously "knocked 'em dead," would usually suggest a particular point on a particular lake, then Dad and Jim would tootle down the bank with their augers and punch some test holes. Whenever we ended up connecting on some fish, I'd look at those three men with frozen-toed reverence. How could *anyone* know where the fish were beneath two feet of ice? How could you look at such a blanched wasteland and decide to drop a line *here*? Eventually I just shrugged it off and equated their woodsmanship with years spent in the field, a heady dose of raw grit, and many, many early mornings spent just like this. I could only hope to reach a similar point someday.

TIME WORE ON, AND AT ABOUT the same rate that I began to hate the practice of ice fishing, I came to fall ass-over-teakettle for another outdoor outlet: trapping.

Dad had been a fur trapper back in the days of the great '70s and '80s fur boom; a time when you could, quite literally, make a fortune peddling furs if you had the know-how and the gasoline. Red fox pelts were kissing a hundred bucks a pop, and even the humble muskrat went north of five dollars. Most of these furs went to the coat industry, which in the United States alone in 1980 cleared nearly a billion dollars. That's *billion* with a 'b.'

It wasn't such a lucrative trade when I took up the reins in 2005, but as a nine-year-old I cared for money about as much as I cared for coffee.

It started not long after we moved from northern Colorado to southeastern Wyoming. The good news about the move was that Wyoming had more space and fewer people. The bad news was that Zeke, our old yellow Lab, finally succumbed to dog years and cancer, and then something started digging up his grave.

It was a bluebird afternoon, just a few days after Hank and I left for school knowing full-well we'd never see Zeke again. I'd just gotten home and had dumped my backpack on the floor. Dad was looking out the kitchen window to the lone cottonwood where Zeke was buried.

"We ought to set some traps up there," he said.

I'd heard Dad mutter about trapping before, and I'd seen old sepia-tinted pictures of his trapline escapades, but the process was foreign and therefore logged as something I probably wouldn't do.

"The coyotes have been messing with Zeke's grave," he added.

That changed some things. I'd never killed anything up to that point besides some of those winter trout and a rooster pheasant, but if you were going to meddle with my dead dog, you could cue the chant from *Lord of the Flies* because I was gonna spill your blood.

As soon as Dad extracted some of his old fox traps from the back of the shed, I went from tepid to totally insane for the idea of trapping. I couldn't press the springs down on my own, and I hadn't the faintest idea of where to put the things in order to catch something, but it didn't matter. In the same way that I've come to be permanently damaged from the punctures of a fish hook, I realize now that all those blood-blisters I got from snapped traps never really went away. My school notes from that era are riddled with ersatz drawings of traps and trap sets. My free time was consumed nearly entirely with trapping literature (S. Stanley Hawbaker became my Messiah), and I pestered Dad relentlessly.

It finally happened on a day in late November; snowless, anemic, blustery. Dad took us out to the north end of our property and set some coyote traps, a process that involved several complicated steps and felt at least partly religious. I hung on to his every word. After that we set some traps along the creek, just for the fun of it, and *whadda ya know*, two days later we pogoed down to find a big ol' male raccoon in one of them.

I still remember exactly how that felt. It was just a 'coon—actually, it appeared more like some ragged, ambiguous thing you'd pull out of a dumpster—but to carry it with Hank up through the sage gullies, back to the four-wheeler and eventually back to Mom who would have the camera ready, was to know pure boyish thrill. It was still dark, but the sun was patiently rising behind gauzy clouds in the east. It started to snow.

From that point on, nearly every morning between November and February (when the furs were prime, as Dad said) was one that began in the dark for me. I have several journals' worth of trapping history from those days, beginning on November 26th, 2005—the day Dad set those first traps—and petering out in the spring of 2014 when I started preparing to leave for college. Through the several hundred pages they encompass, these entries show a kind of naturalist evolution. I got proficient at trapping raccoons and muskrats, I avenged Zeke by catching coyotes, and I eventually cracked the codes of mink and high-country bobcats. I came to understand that "As ye reap, ye shall sow," wasn't just an epitaph from the Good Book; my pleasure in the outdoors was directly proportional to the effort I put in. I also figured out, though, that sometimes you could work your tail off for days, weeks, months even, and your journal entries would still look like this: *November 25th, 2007—Caught nothing.*

Speaking of that 2007–2008 season, it was the first time I really tried my hand at trapping mink. This equated to a lot of aimless walks along the creek, yearning as only a ten-year-old can, tossing and turning at night wondering if the animals existed or not.

Finally, things came together. Maybe the stars tilted just right. The entry from January 10th, 2008 says only, "*I caught my first mink,*" but the picture on the following page, and moreover the memory that's lodged in my soul like a fossil, shows a kid in a red sweatshirt about to self-detonate with joy at the little mink hefted in his uncalloused grip.

WE CONTINUED OUR ICE-FISHING TRADITION into my late teens. Maybe we didn't go *every* year, but we at least thought about it and would go the next year if we missed it. I still never saw Ted and Sue's in the daylight, I still packed as though I was joining Shackleton to the South Pole, and I still sat at the dining table with those three men every morning. The only things that really changed for me between the ages of eight and eighteen were the facts that I, too, would partake in Ted's coffee, and that my sleeping bag slowly, almost imperceptibly, got longer.

Today, rimfire in the backseat and tires thrumming below me toward some prime November hare country, almost twenty years on, their stories seep back. I can hear them: Jim crouched stock-still in a duck blind; Ted punching holes before sunrise to have a shot at that twenty-five-inch trout; Dad readying the mules before the long ride to elk camp.

I sip my coffee like they used to do. Black, strong enough to warp a spoon. They'd drink it and spin their yarns until one of them would clap their knee and together they'd step out under the glowing bone of the moon, out into a darkness as cold as Pluto.

Now looking back, Alaskan winter rushing up the windshield, I realize that Jim's, Ted's, and Dad's stories all had one thing in common: they began and ended in the dark. They all bore passion to beat the sun, and throughout my life I guess I've understood that to be an important thing. And not just for trout or burbot or mink. Somewhere along the line, as I sucked in this truth and came to live by it, I also realized that, like those men, like those lodestars, I had my own tales to share. See the world before the sun and life can be pretty good.

So here they are: my own stories stitched together by how they began and ended and what I can only hope is that same passion to chase the dark and to seek the fins, furs, and flurries of wings beyond it. They might be arranged chronologically and they might not. They might be partially fabricated and they might not, though they're all true.

Let's imagine that we're all seated around a table. It's still dark but we've got time. Maybe Jim's back there frying bacon. We'll step out into the cold soon enough, to hunt hares or ice-fish, and we'll watch our breath vent upwards under a dome of van Gogh stars.

For now, just listen.

BURBOT AGAIN

THIS IS A PLACE WHERE PEOPLE INDULGE in their vices: graffiti, heroin, fornication, burbot. It's tucked out by the end of the airport in Fairbanks, Alaska where a series of levees butt into the Tanana River. Back in 1967, before these levees existed, the Tanana ran free with its feeder the Chena and together they flooded the hell out of the city. 95% of Fairbanks was inundated and $85 million in damages were incurred. Apparently, the city learned its lesson because over the next couple of decades they spent a lot of time hauling gravel and digging dikes along the riverbanks. By the time I showed up for college at the University of Alaska Fairbanks in 2014, I guess you could say the Tanana and the Chena were tamed. Back then I had no idea what kinds of creatures wandered their banks or wiggled beneath their flows, or just how important some of them would become for me.

What I did know is that I wanted to run an Alaskan trapline. Wyoming, where I grew up, and its high-plains quarry were great, but I think there's yet to be a trapper who isn't fascinated by chasing fur in the Far North. I imagined checking traps in the dark before class, lucking into such exotic species as lynx, marten, wolverines, and silver fox.

The August before school started, Dad and I made the 3,100-mile drive from Wyoming to Fairbanks in my cramped little Ford Ranger. There were about two hundred pounds of steel traps in the back. As soon as we hit the city limits, I sniffed out a part-time job at a nearby research farm. I shoveled musk-ox crap and helped artificially inseminate reindeer cows, and somewhere in between I arranged my obligatory college course schedule, secured a trapping license, and researched local maps until I went half-insane.

This was new country, and not just for trapping. For me. Oddly enough, the geography was the easiest element to grasp. I was three thousand miles from the place I grew up in, separated by two time zones and at least half a dozen ecological regions. More unsettling was the pill that I was on my own for the first time in my life; on my own in a way where I couldn't just make a weekend trip to Mom and Dad's to do laundry.

Not only that, but my girlfriend, Emmie, and I were in the same place for more than a week for the first time ever. Our years of maintaining a long-distance relationship were over. We basked in this honeymoon newness until it became routine; then when things started to get snippy, we'd remember what it was like to try to fight over Skype. Usually we'd get over ourselves.

College made me the proverbial fish out of water for a while. I'd been handed good grades in high school because, a.) I wasn't a moron, b.) when I *was* a moron, it normally wasn't at school, and c.) because I possessed an intuitive sense of what every teacher in that building was looking for (except in mathematics—Geometry can go right to hell). Mom called it my "gift of gab." I could wax poetic about ribosomes for ten pages and pull an A out of it, but if you were to ask me to tell you what a subunit did, or to describe tRNA in even the simplest terms, I'd be screwed. This became a problem with college. The ol' gift of gab got me nowhere because college professors saw right through it.

Trapping proved equally difficult at first. I jumped into it like I do most everything else—that is, *naively*—and assumed that, this being Alaska, I'd have a king's share of land to plant my steel upon and, me being unslakable, I'd have my dorm room full of fur by Christmas break. Neither happened.

DESPITE MY SHAKY INTRODUCTION TO THE AREA, Fairbanks turned out to be a good place to spend my college days. It was a city with movie theaters and Thai restaurants and a Barnes & Noble, but once you got to know people it had the chummy feel of a small town. Run into so-and-so at the grocery store. Hear about an accident on the Johansen and know who was driving. Things got familiar.

Trapping improved, too. In my manic map-searching I'd located a patch of state ground that hadn't already been claimed, and initially the catch was good; four marten and a red fox in relatively short order. I smuggled the marten carefully into my dorm room using an oversized backpack, hoisted my bed up on some risers, and skinned my plunders beneath it. It actually worked out pretty well, and though the drying fur took up a lot of space in my already tiny living quarters, there's no feeling more fulfilling than watching fur dry. Of course at one point I had a few fresh skins drying during the week of mandatory room inspections. The skins were flesh-side out and looked rather grotesque, so I left a note (a plea, really) for the residence hall director to not give me the boot. They must not have cared.

Eventually, though, the catch declined. This was dismaying until I figured it out: Alaska, being in northern latitudes, has low and highly-localized densities of furbearers. This means you can stand to catch a few right off the bat if your methods are sound and you're in the right place, but it also means that after a certain point, you'll be trapping a ghost town. You can't catch a clothesline of fur without traveling a hundred miles and, since I was footbound, I didn't stand half a chance of meeting my own expectations. I kept at it year after year, but between rival trappers encroaching on my territory and cyclic animal populations (which I always seemed to catch the downside of), my enthusiasm dissolved. That and my own morality began to creep in.

Catching marten in Conibear traps, which kill their quarry almost instantly, was one thing. No need to feel guilty about that as far as I'm concerned, provided you're setting these traps in ethical ways. But laying foothold traps for fox and lynx, for example, where my target species would theoretically become handcuffed and rendered immobile until such time that I could get there and dispatch them, made me uncomfortable. It made me uncomfortable even when I trapped my heart out in high school, which is why I'd get up at four a.m. to make sure I was checking traps daily.

In Alaska, though, where I was driving ninety miles round trip before or after work and class, it just wasn't possible. The state maintains a ten-day trap check law where you have to tend to your sets at least once in that period. Like I said, the country is big, and some of the serious Alaskan trappers are running two-hundred-mile plus traplines from the backs of snowmachines. They obviously stomach the thought that some of their catches are sitting alive in foothold traps for over a week, but I've no idea how. This is not to tout myself as holier than thou or anything; this is to say that I was experiencing the beginning of the end of my trapping career, and I didn't even know it.

It's funny how stuff like that takes shape. If you'd have told me at the age of eighteen that there would come a winter in which I *didn't* set a trap, I'd have shrugged you off and made damn sure that your prophecy never came true. That's who I knew myself to be; Joe Jackson was a trapper, and would remain one, and someday someone would carve a steel trap into my headstone. Yet as those ideals parted like curtains and let me reflect on my practice and why I did what I did, I found that my aversion to *not* trapping was anesthetized. The world would keep turning. There were other worthy pursuits. By the time I was ready to graduate college three years later, my lust for fur and for endless traplines had settled to a distant hum. I was okay to just let some things be.

Besides, fishing had wheedled its way in as another legitimate outlet for my brainpower (or lack thereof). I'd been fishing since I was knee-high on a tadpole, as they say, and even though my general interest in the pastime never wavered, it did accelerate in those later college days. The timing seemed to work out serendipitously; as I was phasing trapping out, I learned a lot more about fly fishing and how it was supposed to be done. That and I had a whole new place to do it in, a relentless fishing partner called The King (who we'll meet later on), and a smattering of new species to make things exciting. One of those species had absolutely nothing to do with fly fishing, but somehow served to fascinate me more than any other.

Enter the fish with too many nicknames. Enter the eelpout, the mud shark, the lawyer, the cusk, the ling cod, the mother of eels, the loche, the methy, the mariah, the coney fish. Enter the burbot.

SO THERE I AM, FIVE YEARS later—OR IS IT SIX?—out on the south end of the airport on one of those flood mitigation levees that butts into the river and leaves a swirling eddy on its downstream side. The time is somewhere between one and two a.m. Out here with the burbot.

My bleary eyes probe the dark and the moonlight breaks onto the river like a bunch of blue candles. A hungry cold glides across my hands. Soon it will be time to reposition the baits and cut more. Restless ducks chatter where the shadows pool. Restless like me. Here on the river the water wells up as if from the center of the planet, molten and glacial at once, singing with silt and the keels of ice jams.

You fish for burbot the same way you fish for any bottom-feeder: you plunk a bait in a likely spot and wait. Usually, it's good to have something else to do while you're doing this waiting—whittling, identifying birds, and tending a campfire are all good—because you could be waiting a long time. That's how it started out for me. I had at least an academic knowledge about where to find burbot, but the fish themselves were as strange as a coelacanth. I scoured satellite maps—not unlike I'd done with trapping spots—and focused my efforts on the flood levees. I scouted these places well before the ice was out, which was good to get me off campus but really served no purpose. You can't tell much of the river's character beneath a yard of ice. This was around the end of March, which meant I had at least a month to go. And let me tell you: *Nothing* goes so slow as waiting for the ice to go out.

A redeeming virtue of the burbot is that as soon as this ice *is* out, though, you can fish for them. They don't care if the water is gin or a protein shake; they'll feed in it, navigate through it, spawn their horny burbot-y bodies around in it like the world's gonna end tomorrow.

Just like it took me a while to figure out Fairbanks and marten trapping, it took me awhile to find the burbot. It took me even longer to say confidently that I had the fishery 'dialed,' (a term of devoted angling vernacular which here means, "figured out to an extent as to seem competent.") The moment came after several miles of postholing through snow at the end of the airport, many hours of dozing on a riverbank waiting for something to nose my baits, and a not-insignificant chunk of my Calculus class that was spent daydreaming about the burbot's lithe, mottled shape.

Growing up, I fished for carp and catfish in the North Platte River with similar zeal, and as such had a decent resume of bottom fishing credentials. I could launch into a description of my setup, but that would likely bore you as much as Calculus did me, so I will leave it at the essential tool of my methods:

A fishing bell.

The fundamental purpose of the fishing bell is to signal a bite. There's not a steep caloric expenditure required to bottom-fish, which is why you can be a five-hundred-pound diabetic and still enjoy yourself. The inevitable idleness, however, which can stack neatly into hours upon hours of *nothing*, can make even the most focused begin to wane. The fishing bell serves more as an alarm than an indicator; you could be snoozing four beers deep, but when you hear that first tinkling it's like you just got blasted by an AED. Dry-fly fishing or swinging flies for steelhead will get my motor runnin' these days, sure, but nothing will ever match the sudden, profound, and singularly urgent noise of a fishing bell dancing to life.

Speaking of bells, there's one jiggling now. It's dark, not pitch black, but everything is sucked down to shadows. Fairbanks is a noisome cloud of light behind me. The airport sparkles and the world is swallowed by the sound of planes taking off.

Burbot will noodle around with a bait for a while before they swallow it. I move to the rod and put my hand on its cork. I can feel the interest of something on the other end. We use radio signals and infrared waves and ultrasounds to reach out and touch life that's beyond us. Here it's a fishing line. Finally the bell stops. I reach up. I hold the rod and point it in the general direction that I think the fish is, then when I feel the line tighten I strike upward and set the hook.

Weight. Like a two-by-four. Then the lumber stirs to life and so do I, pawing away the sleep in my eyes, new blood washing through me. I could be fishing the North Platte again, hoping that for once this is a catfish, or I could be tromping through the cold of my marten trapline, the first glimpse of fur through the trees as bright as a flare. Heart kicking hot blood. I'm fishing here years after I first discovered the burbot, years after I stooped in the dark and waited for the bells.

The first full night I spent in their pursuit I caught two. They were small as burbot go, but when they surfaced they made waves much bigger. I was hooked by their otherworldly appearance. I was hooked by their repulsive lovability. I was hooked because, like the carp and catfish of days long passed, burbot are questions. They're there and they're not. I finally drove home in a coffee daze that night and took a nap before heading to morning class, where my buddy Logan famously said:

"Joe, it's light here twenty hours a day, and yet you still choose to fish in the dark."

That's how it goes. Waiting for ice-out and leaving the apartment just as Emmie, now my wife, is going to bed. Eyes itching. Coffee and the old flannel jacket that smells like chopped lamprey. Basking not in the light of springtime but in the darkness that stitches it all together.

Others enjoy the dark, too. I'm rarely alone out there. Sometimes someone will light a bonfire and you'll see its jagged primal glow or hear the voices of its occupants. Sometimes people drive up and down the levee roads, so slow it's like they're looking for you, stopping for long periods, eventually disappearing into the gloom. It's not hard to imagine what they're doing out here, not when the evidence of discarded syringes and yellowed condoms pile in the mud like flotsam. Indulging their vices. Letting their spirits crash free and monstrous through the dark.

Burbot fishing is like that, and it isn't. It's not like heroin but it's not *un*like it either, because here I am strung out from no sleep and a touch of selfishness and a reckless pursuit of ... what? A thrill? A question? An escape? Mostly it's just empty time—as empty as shooting up and crashing back down, hollow as an oil drum, a day late and a dollar short. Yet, the action continues. I go to work half-asleep, I daydream like that's my occupation because the thoughts I have at one a.m. are somehow more important than any I could conjure during waking hours. And it's driven by the 'what if'—the grinding river, the creatures beneath it, the high of burbot.

Now, at last, the two-by-four fish has been subdued. I have a look and a thank-you, and at the moment when others would thump the beast over the head with a rock and heft its limped body into a cooler, where others would light up and shoot up and fornicate their heart's desire here under the moon, I let it go.

There's the distant rumble of trucks. A morning call-to-prayer by a Labrador. Fairbanks waking. In a while it will be time to take up the rods, take up the bells, change clothes and go to work. For now, though, here I am in the mud, watching the airplanes, out in this sliver of the world where I once felt lost but no longer. Out here with the burbot again.

FISHING WITH THE KING

THERE I WAS LYING ON MY BACK in an Alaskan trout stream, everything soaked and sore, my finger wrapped in the shreds of a sock and a pilsner-induced hangover dashing circles inside my skull. I didn't start out that way; I began on two feet but, with a rogue step over a cobble, I struck the ground hard on my hip and my sunglasses tumbled end-over-end through the air before becoming lost to the stream, never to be seen again. Ahead of me, the King hardly noticed. His eyes were lasered toward his indicator, which was telling the tale of his salmon egg fly ticking through a likely trout run. He only acknowledged my existence when he set the hook into a brutish fish and shouted, "There's a 'bow!"

Circumstances like that can make you think about returning to the truck and buzzing off to the nearest diner—the nearest anywhere, really—and leaving your partner stranded in what you consider due comeuppance. Their only transgression is making the most of a situation which you feel you pulled the short straw from, of course, but still—it's unforgivable in the moment.

Eventually I wallowed back onto my feet and managed to swoop a net under the King's prize: a stout male rainbow, his scales still clinging to the sanguine luster of the spawn. You've never seen a kid more jazzed than the King with a trout.

Now with the chance for reflection, it's with no hesitation that I point to this fishing trip as "life-changing," (even though the term is pathetically overused to the point of dilution.) People have life-changing events all the time that, really, probably did nothing to alter the course of their sentience. They had a good time—a great time, maybe, or possibly even an awful one—and then they moved on and eventually forgot about it. No; when I say "life-changing" here, I mean that my perspective was irreversibly altered as a direct result of the experience. I saw something in a way that I couldn't unsee. A switch was flicked, a circuit was completed. Amperage filled me that day that hasn't gone away, and I suspect it won't ever.

It sounds melodramatic, I know, but that's just how it was in those two days fishing in the rain. That's how it was fishing with the King.

APPROXIMATELY 0.00016% OF THE WORLD'S POPULATION is from Goshen County, Wyoming. That means that this particular strain of Wyomingite—native to the southeast river basins of the state, familiar with things like sugar beet farming and artificial cattle insemination and pheasant hunting—is just shy of being, literally, one in a million.

The fact that Ryan Kelly and I were part of this same statistic meant that we inevitably played Little League together and attended the same Bible camps growing up. To say that we were childhood friends would be a stretch—Ryan was two grades ahead of me and went to school in the next town over—but to say we were strangers would be blasphemous. Nobody is strangers in Wyoming. What you could say with total certainty, though, was that we'd never fished together. Ryan and his dad and brother were obsessive fly anglers. I was not. My first dabbling at fourteen involved shoddy casts and maddening snarls of fly line. I wasn't chomping at the bit to take trout on a fly; I just did it whenever Mom and Dad offered to drive me anywhere, and I thought it was neat whenever it happened correctly.

I even remained halfhearted with a fly rod after I moved to Alaska in 2014. That sounds like heresy because it is. Here I had virtually boundless streams to learn on, but through a combination of being interested in other things (you know: trapping, burbot fishing), a lack of confidence in myself, and a misguided and altogether-petulant belief that all the good Alaskan fishing had left decades ago, my childhood fly rod sat under my bed collecting dust.

I took it out a few times that first year in Fairbanks. I took it out a few more times after I enrolled in a fly fishing class and some of the nuances of the sport were revealed: how to effectively fish a nymph, for instance, or how to mend line and achieve a drag-free drift. Some of the cogs were fitting together, but still, I wouldn't go so far as to call myself a fly fisherman.

Ryan, on the other hand, had never stopped being one. His path took him to West Point Military Academy straight out of high school, and though most of his time was spent getting shouted at or ironing his bed sheets, I believe Earth's orbit would've been thrown off if he didn't fly fish at least once or twice. Once graduated and a bona fide member of the United States Army, he was sent to Missouri (and brown trout) before receiving his longer-term assignment in 2016:

Fort Wainwright, Alaska. Five miles from the college where I was probably failing a biology test.

Wainwright isn't an uncommon place for fresh Army recruits to end up. The installation began in 1940 as Ladd Airfield, constructed just a few months after a certain war had been declared in Europe. Ladd's initial role was that of cold-weather research facility. Wainwright remains good for this; the Tanana River valley's bone-cracking winter temperatures can reveal lots of problems with otherwise impeccable technology. By 1942, the United States had entered into several Lend-Lease agreements with the Soviet Union, and Ladd became the integral transfer point for defensive favors. We send you planes and artillery, you keep those pesky Nazis from seizing the northern hemisphere. It didn't take long for that arrangement to deteriorate; by 1945 at war's end, the United States and the Soviet Union suspected the worst of one another. We'd just dropped two nuclear bombs on Japan, vaporizing hundreds of thousands of people along with preconceptions of what weapons could be. It was the first time in the history of humanity that we could deal mass destruction on the scale of entire cities with singular weapons. Talk about life-changing.

(Napalm is widely regarded as the original weapon of mass destruction, and in fact killed more people in World War II than did nuclear weapons. In a single night in March 1945, the United States dropped nearly 1,700 tons of napalm bombs on the Japanese city of Tokyo. Over 100,000 people were killed and millions more were left homeless. In the case of the Fat Man nuclear bomb, though, dropped over Nagasaki just five months later, a mere fourteen pounds of plutonium wrought nearly identical damage.)

Anyhow, Wainwright is where Ryan ended up.

Whenever people leave Goshen County, Wyoming, it's a fairly big deal. Seventy percent of my graduating class still lives within a two-hour radius of home. It almost goes without saying that if you do something other than that—like attend West Point or even just get a job in Lincoln, Nebraska—you achieve near-celebrity status. You return home on winter breaks like some pilgrim with war stories. The fact that I'd gone to Alaska had made the paper, for Pete's sake.

That's probably why, when Ryan found out he was going to Alaska, too (albeit for far-divergent reasons), his mom called my mom and my mom called me. Mrs. Kelly, the virtuously caring mother, wanted to know what it was like; what Ryan should be prepared for and how he could avoid freezing to death or succumbing to the soul-rotting darkness of wintertime. I did my best to relay what could pass for advice. Ryan himself wanted to know one thing:

What was the fishing like.

He had this vision of Alaska as a mountainous, trout-filled paradise. Crystal-clear streams with flourishing salmonids crossed the highway at regular intervals, and all you had to do was take one step either upstream or downstream to achieve complete and utter solitude. I think he was describing some Wyoming-Montana hybrid from about a hundred years ago.

I was fiendishly happy to burst his bubble. Fairbanks was a census area of a hundred thousand people, all of whom were probably looking for the exact kind of fishing Ryan had imagined. That and all of these "trout" he pined for weren't naturally found north of the Alaska Range, and most of the "crystal-clear" streams were tannic and therefore the color of tea. Sure, solitude and epic fishing could still be found in the Far North, but it'd take a Cessna, a jet boat, or a small fortune coughed up to someone possessing either of these craft to get there.

"There's not very good fishing on the road system," I whined, which, in my limited experience, was true.

Ryan's inquiries proved relentless, though, and they always contained a "what if."

"What if you hiked six miles downstream."

"What if you got a packraft."

"What if you drove five hundred miles south."

I'd never considered any of these schemes before because I didn't care to. Just because I knew how to fly fish a little better than I did when I left Wyoming didn't mean that I was obsessed with it. I gave Ryan my honest opinions and figured he'd come to terms with his naivety sooner or later (not unlike I'd done with fur trapping). He'd get jaded by the crowds and the tea-stained water and all the driving you had to do just to get anywhere. Then I said good luck and that was that.

I heard from him again in late April. He'd moved up and had already sniffed out a local grayling haunt. I knew about it, but so did everyone in the city of North Pole. I'd never fished it on the theoretical grounds that it was hammered and therefore pointless.

We met up in the late afternoon, after class and after work. We parked on the side of a busy road and cast streamers and nymphs toward a wide, echoing culvert. The water was milky and sluggish; it came from the nearby Chena River and backed up in a kind of slough, which had the happy coincidence of being a prime grayling spawning corridor. And, boy, did we catch them.

I didn't get any indication of Ryan's fishing character that afternoon, except maybe that he just couldn't get enough of it and stayed casting until well after the sun crept away. When I say fishing character, I mean a few things: How hard does someone fish? Do they move quickly or stay in one spot for long periods of time? How many fly changes do they make? How early are they willing to get up? How late do they stay out? What kinds of challenges are they willing to endure for the sake of fish?

These things, beyond fleshing out someone's stance on recreation, can determine the compatibility of a fishing buddy. By that point in my life, I prided myself on the fact that few people could out-fish me. I don't mean "out-fish" as catching a higher quantity (tallies are for losers and tournament anglers), but in being willing to fish longer and harder. Like I said, I wasn't exactly over the moon for fly fishing, and I wasn't convinced of Alaska's angling prowess, but I knew how to treat the whole thing like a job that required overtime. Blame the burbot fishing, I guess. I could stay out as long as it took and then some—at some point, you kind of get stuck and your mind wraps itself around things other than time. Seconds become more chances that stack up like haybales; another cast, a little longer, it's gonna happen sometime. Wait it out.

Ryan seemed to have a similar philosophy, but I couldn't be sure. That first outing together was easy-going; warm, comfortable, no hardship other than mosquitoes. No true colors were really shown and nobody out-fished me.

Man, did that change.

OUR NEXT FISHING TRIP TOGETHER DIDN'T HAPPEN until the following October.

"Wanna try for some cohos?" This was Ryan, with typical Ryan-enthusiasm.

"Where?" This was me, preparing to be reluctant.

Ryan mentioned a river I'd heard about—I'd fished it extensively for grayling, in fact—but even then, the cohos seemed out of my league. Unknown and thereby unattainable. I was content to let them stay there. Ryan wasn't. Next thing I knew we were standing in the dark of pre-dawn with thirty-six-degree water hugging us up to our hips.

I'd never fished the river beyond the campground stretch. Ryan had never fished the river, period, but kept leading the way upstream, bend after bend. Blazing a trail, seemed like. Finally we stopped in a deep U-curve where the water slowed and, it turned out, the cohos liked to hang. Years later I would do extensive research on these fish and find out that they'd come all the way from the Bering Sea, nine hundred river-miles away. The water we stood in hosted the largest run of coho salmon in the entire Yukon River drainage, a watershed roughly the size of Venezuela. This wasn't just a pass-through stream for these fish, either. This was it. The end. "A terminal fishery," in biologist-speak. They'd spawn here and die.

As such, the fish were vividly colored and heroically tired. We caught a few that day and my world was cracked open. These fish *could* be caught. Alaska was a place where you *could* hop into a river and wander to your heart's content. My petulance, my reluctance, my misconceptions began to change colors the way cohos did. My growing familiarity with fly fishing turned to an affinity. And, perhaps most jarring of all, that day was the first time in my life someone clearly out-fished me. I was exhausted—physically, mentally—from fishing with Ryan, and that was just trying to keep up. As the sun extinguished itself behind the spruce tops, he just kept going, and I found myself torn between wanting to hate him and worship him in the same breath.

From that point on, we fished together all that we could. I mean, here I'd been in Alaska for two years, and it took Ryan the newcomer to show me some of the place's lordliest fish. He challenged me; he pushed me to my limits. All I did for him, probably, was share in the gas expenses.

So—there we were on the trout stream where our story began, me lying sore and drenched in the riverbed, Ryan hooked up to an acrobatic fish. We'd been fishing since four a.m. when, tired and sore and migrained, we'd crawled out of a rain-drenched tent, piled it in a tangle in the back of the truck, and started hiking through veritable rainforest. Ryan's creek—as it was known to me then—was a small salmon-spawning stream in the Susitna watershed. Being small and conducive to salmon sex, it was rich in nutrients and thick with foliage and bears. These problems required antidotes; hearty expletives for the maddening wickerwork of bankside alders, firepower in the form of a .44 Magnum for the members of the *Ursus* genus. (Luckily I've never needed to fire that thing).

The evening before, we'd made the long drive south from Fairbanks, passing from the flattened river valleys of the Interior to the lofty forests and crashing rivers of Southcentral. We swung flies for cohos at the mouth of a nearby river until past midnight. Ryan landed a silver and I netted a beastly ten-pound chum that thrashed so violently it dealt several cuts on my hands. Hence the shreds of sock wrapped tourniquet-like on my fingers the following day. Dirtbagger first-aid. We celebrated Ryan's coho with pilsners and set up a hasty camp in a growing downpour.

Now, back on two feet after my unintended somersault, rain sheeting off me, I readied the net. Ryan played the trout like he knew what he was doing—which, of course, he did—and every time it would jump he'd whoop and laugh his head off. Like a kid who just won a baseball trophy. Like a kid who just won the world.

Just as the atomic bomb shattered the human conception of weapons in 1945, that trout took my relationship with fly fishing and blew it out of proportion. I mean it. Just like that. Sounds like more melodrama, I know, but again, it's justified. It was a twenty-one-and-a-quarter-inch male rainbow, spotted like a jaguar, and I can see him now six years later as clearly as I did then. His dorsal fin was split and weathered. There was a divot in his bony upper jaw, a feature of genetics, maybe, or an old hook scar. Ryan stood over it saying nothing. I like to imagine now that a flash of time was trundling behind his eyes; the reckoning of all the early mornings and late nights he'd spent on that stream just trying to figure it out. After all, it appears modest from the road. So modest that I'd never even considered there'd be fish in it; if you'd have asked me about it—and Ryan did one time—I'd have told you it probably wasn't worth it. Yet Ryan had gone and scoured books and found out how to access it, and with his hallmark "What Ifs" and titanium insatiability, he'd learned how to catch its residents. Blazed a trail right through it. The creek gets a run of all five Pacific salmon, but, more intriguing, it harbors some epic rainbow trout.

You had to get up in the dark to attain its spoils. You had to be the first one on the stream. In water that tight the trout were spooky, so the first casts through likely runs would be the best. You had to fight the brush and you had to brave the ever-present danger of bears. You had to bring a backpack with enough water and food and extra layers to last a day, because this wasn't a stream to dangle your toes in for an hour. You hiked three miles to the mouth and back and you "fished your balls off," as Ryan would say, every minute in between. Dawn to dusk.

(Ryan didn't coin the term "fishing your balls off," but as far as I know, he's the most consistent practitioner.)

I looked hard at that trout, and I looked hard at this fellow Little Leaguer and Goshener that had caught it. He seemed to have fly fishing and, somehow, life all figured out. I wanted what he had.

Not just in singularity, either. I wanted it forever, long as I lived. Here was the fruition of Ryan's effort, not *the* end, but *an* end, and a fitting one. This was a man who'd asked a question, fought the alders and the bears and the rain for an answer, and had received one. One that couldn't be seen from the road.

There was no half-in, half-out with fly fishing. There was no room for indifference or petulance or reluctance; if you were gonna do it, you did it, and you did it at your limits, whatever those were. You did it with a headache and you did it hypothermic and you did it with a sock tourniquet wound down around your finger. You got up at three a.m. to be first on the stream. You fished hard all you could and you kept the faith like a totem and you held it close because—well, I guess I don't really know why. Seemed important, though. Still does.

"Good fish, rainbow king," I said, still gawking at the trout.

I remember the fish and I remember my words.

Rainbow King.

Ryan scoffed it off and released the fish and, seconds later, was back to eagle-focus. It can't have been ten more casts that he hooked up to another trout. I followed him like that the rest of the day, into the night, and again the next. We caught lots of trout, lost lots, too, and with each fish and each bend, I fell more hopelessly in love. With trout. With fly fishing. With asking questions of streams and seeking the answers. I kept the faith, tucked it in my hat like a feather, and if I ever started to ask why, I'd be reminded by a yank on the rod and the startling, leaping fight of a fish. The explosion of senses. The spectacular blinding corona, not of fission, but of trout.

Ryan would go on to relocate to Missouri with his family that next spring, and move to Kansas a few years after that. The Rainbow King in Kansas; I'm still wrapping my head around that one. But before he did any of that, before our paths split, we spent one last September day on his creek. We got up at two in the morning to make the drive from Fairbanks. We drank coffee and talked about fish won and lost, about God. We saddled up under the haunting glow of headlamps. We fished our balls off.

I caught the biggest rainbow trout of my life that day—the biggest two, actually—and despite Ryan snapping his rod about a mile down the creek (requiring a hike *back* to the truck in order to continue fishing), you couldn't write a better day. We both knew it would be Ryan's last trip on the stream, at least for the foreseeable future—Missouri called as Alaska once had—so we fished slow and carefully and tried to breathe it all in. I may have gotten tired or impatient as I watched Ryan make cast after cast, or as he'd hike up and down and back up again just to fish the logjam one more time, or as I'd have to go dashing after him as he steered a lively trout downstream, but I didn't say anything. I knew I was living a day I'd remember forever, like that cold October one chasing cohos, like that rainy one in August just a few weeks prior. I knew I'd succumbed fully to the King's disease.

That September day at lunchtime, I revealed two bottles of beer I'd carried all the way down the stream in my backpack. They were heavy for a lot of reasons. We cracked them open, just us and Alaska, all around, the memories drifting like fog: the dark shapes of trout tucked under cutbanks, too clever, too lithe to be salmon; the clammy grit of early mornings; the electricity that flowed through our spines. The trout-of-a-lifetime I lost at the net, then hooked in the same exact spot a few hours later and managed to land. Ryan's twenty-seven-incher. His broken rod. All of it.

"To the Rainbow King's last stand," I said.

Rainbow King. Started as a joke, grew to a term of endearment. Now it's a tribute.

We clinked our bottles and drank them and when we were finished I pounded the bottlecaps into a log with a rock. Last I checked, just this past fall, they were still there.

DISPATCHED TO GOLD CREEK

IT'S REMARKABLE NOT HOW QUICKLY the stuff that changes your life can take shape in your mind, but how slowly. Emmie—my wife, my best friend, my cause for optimism—called me on an otherwise bland evening a few Marches ago and heaved a lungful of words that I still hear today:

"I was in an accident. I think my arm's broken."

That was all she could say before the EMTs got her in an ambulance, and I spent the next hour in radio silence. She was in Juneau working for the Alaska State legislature, I was in Anchorage preparing for the final quarter of a secondary teaching internship, and the six hundred miles between us dulled whatever response I could muster. *Emmie was in a car wreck.* At first, the thought was about as ordinary as the internet going out or the cat hacking on the carpet; an inconvenience held at arm's length from true catastrophe only in the way you perceive it. Then it grew, insidious like hypothermia, and by the time it really hit—the way something like that is *supposed* to hit—I was shaking in the glow of airline tickets.

Emmie was in a car wreck.

It's nearly midnight before I got the whole story, which was remarkably short: some girl ran a stop sign. Emmie slammed on the brakes and made a tremendous T-bone and the airbags burst and along with them her wrist. And man, it couldn't be worse timing. Not only would I be returning to teaching in a physical classroom in five days (for the first time in six months thanks to the virtual classrooms of the COVID pandemic), but Emmie was obligated to house-sit for a woman with an atrociously energetic yellow Lab named Finn. Try doing that with a bum arm. I got the next flight out to Juneau.

Juneau weather is usually about as appealing as a wet gym sock. You could say the same about most of southeast Alaska, of course, but Juneau seems especially bad. Even in summer the nice day is rare. This is how a typical conversation goes:

Juneau Guy 1: How was your summer?

Juneau Guy 2: Nice. We went camping that day.

And so on.

I picked Emmie up from the hospital in a fresh rental car thumped with rain, spent about an hour or so on the phone with insurance, and met Finn the Labrador. Our introductory walk didn't go so well. Sure, I grew up with Labs, but the cure for their bottomless energy was to take them out gopher trapping for a few hours or run laps with them on the four-wheeler. None of it involved city sidewalks, and certainly none of it involved cleaning up what came out their back end with my bare hands and a doggy bag. I can put up with a lot in the 'gross' department—liquified raccoon fat and rotting snapping turtle skulls, for example—but the sight, the stench, the *squish* of a steaming dog load is enough to make me gag. Also, whenever people stoop down to collect a pet's deposit, we lose a shred of dignity that we never get back. The thought that I had joined these pathetic ranks was almost too much to handle. It didn't help that Finn ignored the purposes of his training choke collar and towed me around like a tug boat. We returned to the house royally irritated with one another.

It didn't take long for me to feel bad about my raised voice and choice words, though. Finn is, after all, merely a victim of his species and his gender, and I had been frustrated more with the fact that Labradors have no business being contained within city limits than with Finn himself. In truth, I was probably only frustrated with my own circumstances; wife in a car wreck, the morass of insurance dead-ahead, a sixth grade class less than a week away that I still hadn't prepared for—basically the perfect storm for a dog like Finn to become my emotional punching bag. He was quick to forgive me, however, and was even nice enough to introduce me to a pretty little stream called Gold Creek.

I HADN'T HAD MUCH TIME TO GET ANTSY about fishing. It was about halfway through March when all of this went down, which, in a typical year, is about the time that my cabin fever has risen to full swell and presents a danger to myself and others. But teaching, just by sheer nature of how busy it keeps you on a daily basis and how much emotional energy it leeches away, proved an effective antidote. That's not to say I didn't blow off my share of planning time by tying flies or researching the best rod and reel combos for bonefish, but it did feel a bit more like fishing season was sneaking up on me rather than me beating down its door like usual.

Sometimes I lament the limitations of Alaska. You can only (reliably) fish for about five months of the year, and the rest of the time you're squandered by three feet of snow and perpetual darkness and wishing you could be one of those blokes that fishes year-round. The more I think about it, though, I realize that I appreciate fishing more because I can't do it all the time. The adage "Make hay while the sun shines," takes on a whole new meaning in the Last Frontier, and burning gas to capitalize on the limited resources of time and fish feels more workmanlike than it probably would otherwise. And as much as I don't like to admit it, it is nice to have an off-season.

All winter I'd been planning my first fishing trip of the year: steelhead in mid-April. I'm not going to say where. There's usually open-water fishing (some of it purportedly *very* good) to be had on the Kenai, but for some reason casting before April feels to me like false-starting in an Olympic sprint. March is still the province of winter, snowshoe hares, and woodstoves.

After the steelhead, I'd drive north to try and intercept some Susitna rainbows as they moved out of their wintering rivers and into their summer creeks, and as the runoff went down and the waters cleared, the regular season would be *on*. Beyond that, things were vast and uncharted. I had a list of streams and roads I wanted to explore—including a highly cryptic fall run of steelhead on the fringes of one of the greatest wilderness expanses on Earth—and some goals to seek out, but lately I'd sort of learned to let the chips fall. Trying to abide by an itinerary in fishing, or to create one in the first place, is about as effective as trying to steer a king salmon on a five-weight.

All of this jabbering is to say that, no, when I hopped on a plane to Juneau and sat with Emmie through a day of wrist surgery, I wasn't really thinking about fishing.

It's a crapshoot to say what I *was* thinking about during that time, but regardless, it was punctuated by having to walk Finn at least four times a day. Any less than that, I'd discovered on the first night, and he'd sit at the top of the staircase and bark at the moon.

Our walks got better with time. I learned to take him uphill as often as possible to steadily squeeze him into exhaustion. Juneau is a good place for this kind of thing being that it's built into a mountainside. We'd go over past the Governor's Mansion (where the same people sporting "Recall Dunleavy" bumper stickers would be encouraging their Schnauzers to crap in the lawn), then we'd cross the street and climb a rickety metal staircase to the top of the hill.

In between heaved breaths and the kettledrum thump of my own pulse, I'd wonder how in the world people could stand to live here. Houses were literally propped on top of one another; not quite like Hong Kong, but definitely off-putting when you remember that you're in Alaska. Even houses on flat ground were so close that you could read the directions of your neighbor's hemorrhoid medication from the living room window.

Finn and I began to seek out the paths less traveled as we became more familiar with the city. Not only was I sick of having to walk by people on the sidewalk (or worse, see them gawking back at me in their underwear from the kitchen), but if Finn took a dump in the forest and no one saw it, I could just leave it there to dissolve and trickle its way into the water table.

It was during a morning venture like this that we came upon Cope Park, a nice little area with gazebos, a tennis court, and trails slinking off into the vacuum forests of Sitka spruce. Most intriguing about the place was the creek that ran through it. Joe Juneau and Richard Harris discovered gold up this creek in 1880 (or, rather, were shown where the gold was by Tlingit Chief Kowee), and the resulting boom is why Juneau stands today. These days, in the mile-or-so up from where it meets the ocean, Gold Creek is about as lovely as a sewer in Cleveland. It's been contained to a cement sluiceway decorated with the urban trappings of graffiti and litter. Up in Cope Park, however, the creek is held back by a dam, everything upstream of which is composed of gorgeous pocket water that just tugs at your heart.

Finn and I moseyed down here one morning where, just above the dam in a sluggish pool, I spotted a pair of trout-like shapes glued to the bottom. I wanted them to be coastal cutthroats, but careful study of some old Fish & Game records suggested that they were more likely Dolly Varden. They *might've* been brook trout, but the odds were astronomical being that the creek had only been stocked with a handful back when John Bonham was still alive. One was perhaps twelve inches long, the other about eight, and both were resting in water that might've been over my head. Yet I could see them with perfect clarity.

Just as Finn was starting to get antsy about standing still for so long, I started envisioning what kind of a setup I'd use to catch one of these rogues. As a test, I hucked a small pinecone about twenty feet upstream of the fish. It took all of two seconds before both of them dashed to parts unknown. Spooky, alright.

Higher up in the watershed, the long, dammed pool became replaced by plunge pools, quick tailouts, and slicks the size of baking sheets; the high-mountain stream of dreams (although it was maybe a hundred feet above sea level). In this stretch, you might have a second or two for any fish to see your fly, after which point it would be whisked away by the relentless chromium babble.

The Aak'w Kwáan (Tlingit) people call this place Dzantik'i Héeni, or "the creek where little flounders gather." Interpretive signs in Cope Park indicate that, prior to the mining days, the Gold Creek estuary was five feet lower than it is today. The city of Juneau is built on a heroic pile of mining waste. Gold Creek once braided beneath Sitka spruce far taller than any of the multilevel parking garages that live there now.

On our way back to the house, Finn and I stopped to look for the fish again. The pool was bounded on one side by sheer bedrock cliffs, and on the other by the sidewalk upon which Finn and I stood. There was a little maintenance shack further down where, presumably, some guy from the city could turn a little crank and adjust the flow from the dam. You'd have to stand on the sidewalk to make a good cast, but that wouldn't be a problem because the two fish seem to favor a little scar in the creekbed no more than fifteen feet out. You could crouch behind the chainlink fence for a bit of camouflage. I'm thinking something like a size 18 Serendipity, something bright but small enough to alight on the water and dive without causing ripples. You'd probably have to forego the indicator here and fish by sight. What would really be great would be to make the cast with a fiberglass four-weight—Finn drags me onward.

It was a few days later before Emmie felt well enough for me to show her Gold Creek. Even without her accident, that woman is the toughest person I know. Over the last three years, she'd endured months of being alone in this place and navigating the subtle and aggravating hierarchies of politics. In the summertime she'd operate—still does—with a tenacity to rival Finn himself, chasing brides and grooms with her flourishing wedding photography business.

Of course it made me feel sick to see her in a cast, to watch her wince at every tiny movement in her left arm, but at the same time it made me thankful beyond reckoning that I wasn't seeing her in a casket.

You can wander those kinds of corners at a time like that, turning over all the rocks and watching the dark shapes that crawl out from beneath them. Emmie is my entire world. Without her, I'm a river dried up and reduced to a slag pile. I guess that's why they say love is dangerous.

Emmie and I met on a tour bus in Washington, D.C. It was parked outside of a hotel in a downpour, waiting to haul a bunch of teenagers to the Lincoln Memorial. The driver looked as thrilled as if he were about to shoot himself in the face. I know this because I was one of the teenagers flooding past him, as was Emmie.

The whole thing was one of those educational conferences that all seem to have buzzwords like 'Leadership' or 'Youth' thrown into their titles, but which are actually nothing more than pubescent bonanzas in which the hotel rooms are paid for by people you'll never meet. Officially, it was the National Rural Electric Cooperative Association Youth Leadership Conference, in which a handful of high-school-aged students from each state went to learn about—geez, I don't even remember what.

Anyway, Emmie went for Alaska and I went for Wyoming, and we ended up sharing a row on that bus because we were both late and there were only two seats left.

I suppose there are a few moments in every person's life in which, looking back, we wish we could slap our past selves upside the head and tell them to pay attention. That's how it was getting onto that bus; I wish I could swat the flat-brimmed hat off of ol' Joe's head and say, "You're about to meet your wife, you moron. Don't do anything stupid." Naturally, 'stupid' was my modus operandi then and now, but apparently it made no difference because Emmie and I began and held up a long-distance relationship for two years, spent college together in Fairbanks, and got married in June of 2018. I guess, then, it's not entirely fair to say that I learned nothing from the National Rural Electric Cooperative Association Youth Leadership Conference . . . I learned that God *did* make decent women aside from my mother, that approximately one quarter of a good relationship may be destined but the rest of it is good old hard work, and that falling in love with Emmie was, as I would've said back on that tour bus, the "bee's knees."

I'd thought about that day a lot on my walks with Finn. I thought, too, about how pathetic I felt given that I didn't have a paying job and was stuck in three more months of my teaching internship. It's not that I didn't like the teaching, I just didn't like that Emmie was shouldering the weight of providing all by herself. I wanted one of those damn novels I'd spent all that time writing to sell. I wanted an advance check and I wanted to buy Emmie a house where she could pick her own furniture, work in her own kitchen, look out her own windows. I wanted to build her a pottery studio and an outdoor pizza oven. We'd live how we wanted to, far outside of any semblance of a city, far enough to where we could get a Labrador and not feel guilty about it. I guess I knew exactly how Finn felt in those days; I wanted to yar on the leash for all I was worth.

When I showed Emmie the fish in Gold Creek, she didn't see them at first. To be fair, they're the same drab color as the bottom, and even their shape isn't far from an oblong rock or a stick. Maybe I'd been looking for them before I even saw them. When she finally noticed them, though, she made a comment you rarely want to hear about a fish:

"They're so cute!"

Cute was a word for them, sure, but I preferred something like *steadfast*, *valiant*, or *rebellious*. They were, after all, existing in a place maybe they shouldn't have been. More than half of their watershed had been bounded on all sides by Quikrete, and with a century-and-a-half of people messing about in their affairs, you had to wonder how the entire population hadn't gone to a miner's fry pan. But there they were, defying expectation like all good fish do, living their lives and caring not for the anthropic events of car accidents, dog crap, or steady employment. Maybe I'm buying into it a little too much, but I think they portend a bright season ahead. A bright life.

Emmie carries a scar but that's all it will ever be. I never saw Finn again after that week, nor will I ever, probably, but I like to think that he's still out there hauling someone off their feet down the streets of Juneau.

GOD SAVE THE WHITEFISH

THE VERDICT EVERYWHERE WAS THAT SPRING was late. We're talkin' mid-May before the snow really started to melt. The thing about spring in Alaska, though, is that it doesn't take long once it starts. Canadian geese arrive first in pairs, then in squadrons. One day you feel a twinge to go fishing, the next it's grown to an ache.

Acting on such an impulse, I planned a quick weekend excursion. It would begin on a Thursday afternoon right after school let out and end the following Sunday, and would take me on a tour of the Alaskan road system. Only about 20% of the state is even accessible by roads in the first place, but I was going to cover a good chunk of it. The initial impetus was needing to retrieve a large chunk of footage for a video editing job, which was stored in a series of ones and zeros on a server in Fairbanks. It didn't take long for other motivators (shaped like fish and like mayflies), to sweeten the deal.

Altogether the trip would be roughly eight hundred miles. I wasn't sure exactly what those eight hundred miles would be composed of, but I figured I could do worse than just seeing where the fishing took me.

I LIKE DRIVING. YOU KIND OF HAVE TO in this state. I especially like leaving the city and feeling the road get slower and more docile. The traffic lights and car horns turn to ramshackle cabins and lonely stretches of highway broken only by the occasional milepost marker. The only problem is that to get to this state of sedation from Anchorage, heading north at least, one has to go through Wasilla.

Wasilla marks the boundary between urban and rural, and driving through it feels a bit like being forced through a sphincter. There's really only one road in or out, and the air you inevitably become stuck in is a sickening swill of diesel fuel and Mountain Dew. Sometimes you'll see people driving four-wheelers through McDonald's parking lots, and other times you'll see trucks with excessively compensatory lift-kits (compensating for what, you tell me) sporting trailer hitch ornaments that look like steel testicles. You can see that kind of crap elsewhere, sure, but in Wasilla you can almost bet on it. Most of the stop signs have bullet holes in them and even some of the traffic lights do.

The road between there and my first fishing stop is basically the same as I left it the previous October. Someone had spray-painted an account of their love story on a train overpass at some point in the past—"I love you, Rose," and "Rose, my soul-mate,"—and as I go under this time I can see it's been updated:

"Rose, I'm sorry I slept with your sister."

There's even the same guy sitting in the same duct-taped camo overcoat at the same dilapidated camper just outside of Willow. He's got a can of beer in one hand that flashes brilliantly in the sun, and I can only assume he overwintered in this exact position. Some things never change.

One of the campgrounds I intend to stay at is closed when I arrive. Won't open until the next weekend. I cross the highway and check the other. A young girl, maybe eleven or twelve, is painting wooden benches and informs me that they, too, are closed. She's sweet and awkward and reminds me of one of the sixth-grade students I teach. After a little prodding she finds her aunt, who'd clearly partaken in methamphetamines or opioids recently. You try not to judge the book and all that but I mean this gal was strung out like a freakin' clothesline. She tells me that I can have a tent site for the night. As I pick a spot and park and slip into waders, I wish the young girl, who's returned to painting benches, the best. I really do. A future that takes her wherever she wants it to, probably far from here.

I cross the road on foot and plan to fish downstream. The gravel they spread during winter crackles beneath my boots. Having learned a bit about kids in the last year and all the—pardon me—*shit* they have to deal with, I've realized that they're just like this highway. They seem wild and free, at least idealistically, but then you look closer and see all the trash on their shoulders, most of it cast off by adults. Blackened scars sprout upon their skins like cuts and like bruises. One girl in my social studies class has a father that's addicted to pornography. They go, as a family, to therapy every week. A different kid watched his grandma die next to him in a car wreck. I know all that. Can't unknow it.

That night I slept beneath the Tonneau cover in the bed of my truck, tucked between the spare tire and wheel well in an uncomfortable space I've come to refer to as my 'Trouter's Sarcophagus.' I'd fished until dusk.

Terns hovered like kites around me down on the river, occasionally dive-bombing an unseen target like, well, a *tern*. We've got all these gizmos like radar and supersonic fighter jets and autonomous drones—I say "we," but of course the Air Force keeps most of it under tight wraps—but the fact is, we have yet to build something as deadly as the Arctic tern. Just getting to watch them and listen to them is the ultimate consolation prize of spring fishing. They seemed unconcerned by my presence.

MORNING GREETS ME WITH A HEADACHE. Dehydration and too few REM cycles. I crawl and stumble around in the clammy darkness and manage to get wadered up, then I sit in the truck with the heater at full blast and wait for dawn.

I don't recall what I was thinking about, but whatever it was, it was half-formed and brilliant in the way that early morning thoughts can be. For now let's say I was thinking about church and the fact that I hadn't been to a service in over a year. I'm not a total heathen and I don't dislike church, it's just that, for me, organized religion has become a bit like trying to fit into someone else's pants. It's uncomfortable for a lot of reasons, most of which probably stem from my profound introversion. It begins when you walk through the doors. No, I don't want to be greeted by fifty-seven different people all wearing the same expression, just like I don't want to shake that many hands. I also don't want to be cornered by the small-talkers on my way to the seat farthest from the front. Yes, the weather *has* been crazy and, no, much as you think I do, I don't care that your son Huxley got a new saxophone. The whole thing becomes aggravating and before I know it my blood pressure's risen and I'm not retaining a word that the pastor (the only person I *want* to listen to) has said.

Maybe I'm making excuses. I'm good at that. I know God exists and I thank Him every day for the life He's given me, and continues to give me, it's just that I'd rather talk to Him myself without all of the artifacts of church.

People say that this conversation happens through the Bible. (One pastor at childhood Bible camp called it the "instruction manual," and said we ought to read it in order to fix ourselves; same way you'd read an old Ford manual to fix your pickup. Then he told us ten-year-olds about how great sex after marriage was.) While I certainly don't disagree with the assertions about the Bible, I think God speaks in other ways, too. Joseph Heywood once said: "Church is where you find it." Seems to me that I've found it mostly where other people aren't.

I think He spoke to me through the cow moose that wandered down the railroad tracks that morning. I'd gotten out of the truck and hiked a ways toward the creek, and all of a sudden there she was, caught in the limelight of dawn, as beautiful as anything I've ever seen. I watched her for a while, fly rod in hand, unsure of what she could be saying to me other than that life is worth living. Now that I consider it with a bit more clarity, perhaps that was her only message. It's a heavy one, after all.

At another creek farther north, the water was high but clear enough to give me hope. I fished a Kiwi Muddler on a sink-tip, but in perhaps a mile of stream I didn't hook, see, or otherwise have an indication of fish. What I did see was a pair of Harlequin ducks tucked up in a set of turbulent rapids, which jived with observations from previous years but still carried an air of unbelievability. Harlequins are birds that defy logic with their beauty. The males look like something a French monarch would've worn to dinner in the 16th Century: all pewter-gray with accents of mahogany and navy-blue and strokes of white so clean they had to have been made by a paintbrush. There's no way these animals are so pretty just for the sake of reproduction—maybe the message there is that life can be stunning for no reason.

Later, I'll consider God in the chaotic geology of the Denali Fault near Healy, where the rocks are said to be something like 250 million years old. I believe it. But you go spouting that figure within shouting distance of a Baptist church, say, and you'll be flayed alive. The Earth's only supposed to be ten thousand years old, hard max, if God made it. But here's the thing: I don't think God is under any obligation to show his work or somehow prove that carbon-dates and those gleaned from the Bible match up. I take the science and the scripture in one hand. The Earth may be 4.5 billion years old and it might be ten thousand. To pretend to know such a figure is to pretend to know what He is and how He operates, which is laughable. Absurdly so. You can have an idea, sure, just like you can have an idea why fish behave the way they do, but you'll never have answers. Why would you want them, anyway?

I sat there in my church at an easy sixty-five, the radio low, thinking about the moose and the Harlequins and the rocks. The best part was that I didn't have to greet anyone, nor did I have to feign interest in Huxley's new saxophone.

I ARRIVED AT A SPRING CREEK IN DELTA JUNCTION later that afternoon. I stopped in Fairbanks to retrieve the video footage and give the road trip some semblance of purpose. On the way out of town I saw a Lamborghini. I'm not kidding. I've only seen two of these Italian thoroughbreds in my life, and both were in places you'd never expect them: Edmonton, Canada, and Fairbanks, Alaska. That's not to say the exceptionally wealthy can't live above the 49th parallel or anything, but it still makes your jaw go slack when you witness this lavish standard of living. It's hard not to wonder what it'd be like if *I* had that kind of money. Anyway, the car was a Huracan Spyder, and the old guy driving it actually did so pretty casually until he saw an opening in front of a propane truck and stepped on the gas. For a split second those twelve cylinders yelped—sort of like a wild horse just bitten by a rattlesnake—and the next thing I knew the pearly-white beast blasted into hyperspace and out of my life.

Delta Junction was more tame.

I pulled into the campground along my selected creek (one of my favorites in the world), found a good tent site tucked away in the trees, and paid the camping fee. There are a number of spartan campgrounds like this around the state, and their usage fees are among the few in the world that I don't mind paying. Day parking is five bucks (unless you have an annual pass), and camping is twenty. Most of the sites have a fire pit and a bench and that's it. Anything more would attract the wrong kind of people.

In a normal year—here I go assuming that Mother Nature follows a calendar again—the grayling here will be feeding on a menu of caddis and mayflies. I've caught them as early as the last week of April. Most of them will have spawned elsewhere and will be moving into their summer feeding lanes, and though there won't be a lot of fish, there will be a few. You'll find them scattered alongside the giant schools of whitefish that turn up at the same time.

I clomp down the goat trails that eventually peter out past the campground, where the Interior Alaskan taiga is broken by a sweeping lawn as green as anything in suburbia. The lodge here is a gorgeous log structure with a deck, wide windows, and the inviting air that makes you want to stop in for a burger and a malted milkshake after a day of fishing. When I look up, though, the lodge is burnt to the ground; its once golden-ale logs are now the color of charcoal, eaten to nothing, its wide windows burst from the heat, the concrete foundation skeletal like something caught in a war. If I paid attention to any sort of local news, I probably would've known about this before. The Clearwater Lodge, as it was known, burned down back in 2014, but the owners had enough gumption to rebuild. Some quick reading on my phone turns up that it burned down—again—last September.

Fishing the riffle below the lodge is a little depressing, so I continue against the stream. In Alaska, I can follow the watercourse even if the adjacent property is private so long as I stay below the high-water mark. It's as much of a saving grace as it sounds. The only problem here is that the same subterranean aquifers that make this such good grayling habitat also mean that the flow is steady, meandering, and hard to walk against. After a typical day of fishing my honey holes—some as far as two miles upstream from the campground—I feel like I've done one too many leg presses.

The first fish I see are whitefish, the dirty-sequined cousins to the grayling that school up by the dozens and exhibit the sagacity of even the wiliest trout. That's not a joke. They spook at the slightest disturbance and refuse to eat pretty much anything. I'm not sure if it's because they're more interested in reaching their spawning grounds or what, but you'll see them stare down a nymph—even something as small and innocent as a #18 Pheasant Tail—and turn away with the disgust of a vegan in a slaughterhouse. For how lowly the whitefish's reputation often is, they can humble an angler right to his shoes. That's what they did to me that afternoon. I guess in that respect they're a lot like carp.

The church of my youth, aside from the Bible camp previously mentioned and the Baptist chapel that we'd sometimes go to on Sunday mornings, was the North Platte River. And I know what you're thinking. No—I didn't live in the famous stretch of Miracle Mile or Gray Reef where fat browns and rainbows exist in ubiquity. I lived two reservoirs below that, where the targets were creek chubs, white suckers, and common carp. I learned to fish for and appreciate these species mostly because there wasn't anything else. This was around the time that I started watching Jeremy Wade's show on Animal Planet called *River Monsters*, so I was all swollen with the unknown and thinking that there were monster fish lurking just below what I could see. In those days I talked to God about what I was going to do with my life; what it meant to be a kid and then a young man. Maybe I didn't do much listening. I kept my beliefs about science close to the chest because I thought it could only be one or the other.

I bait-fished with raw shrimp, and between early middle school and my graduation from high school, I racked up some impressive carp and had the river figured out in a fifteen-mile stretch near home. Nearly every summer evening was spent somewhere along its length, waiting for the rod to twitch, watching nighthawks skate across the dying sky.

I like to think that it was here that I learned to appreciate nature for what it was rather than what I was told it should be. The carp, for example, was not the "trash fish" that everyone said was better off rotting on the bank; it was a keystone species in that watershed (albeit an invasive one) that cleared algae and provided forage for half the food chain. I can't say this with anything beyond anecdotal evidence, but it seemed that wherever the carp were especially abundant and large, the aquatic diversity was elevated, as well. Smallmouth bass. Walleyes. Rainbow trout. It was also here that I learned that fishing was a far more enjoyable pastime than sneaking around and indulging the teenage sirens of alcohol and fornication. I made it through with a steady girlfriend (now my wife), and the only substance I came close to getting hooked on was Arizona Sweet Tea, so I think I came out ahead.

Back in the campground, I set up my tent and pondered. It was clear that spring was later than usual here just like everywhere else, and that probably explained why all of the boats I'd seen were headed downstream and not up. Maybe the fish just hadn't made it this far yet.

Around me the campground buzzed like a state fair. Popping fires, clattering camper doors, scraps of conversation spilling through the trees. A pair of boys, maybe thirteen years old, walked past my truck. One carried a fishing rod.

It became clear that neither intended to catch a fish, but were instead dipping away from their families to practice some newly-learned vocabulary. They set up shop just below my campsite and, for the next fifteen minutes or so, every other word out of their mouths was an expletive that I'd only repeat under the most dire circumstances—missing a fish or popping a tire, perhaps. It was impressive just how well they could spin these phrases together, and though I'm sure they thought they were vocalizing with a certain degree of stealth, I'm positive that wherever their mothers were, they could hear every word and were generating a tally. Eventually I heard a snap and within moments the pair of them were trudging back down the gravel road.

"How'd ya do?" I asked.

The shorter of the two didn't even hesitate. "The God-damned line broke."

Just like the campground girl three hundred miles behind me, just like any one of my students whose surface trivia I might know, but in whose tiny shoes I could never hope to walk again, I wished them well.

THAT NEXT MORNING, I SLEPT IN, packed away the tent, and enjoyed a cheery few hours of sunshine and boreal owls. My usual spot about a mile upstream produced nothing, but as I waded a section I call "Barking Dog Run" (for reasons that came from a chain-link kennel) I began to see fish everywhere. These were just whitefish, but I stood heron-still and decided to try and catch one. If anything, it'd be a good excuse to scan the vicinity for grayling. I'd abandoned the indicator and had only the faint glint of my bead-headed fly to follow. This was total sight-fishing, excruciatingly so. Cast after cast, me feeling progressively dumber as the fish evaded me. Eventually one of them swallowed the nymph and surprised the hell out of me. It came begrudgingly to the net and I studied it a moment. Whitefish. Beady-eyed.

I clomped back up to the campground after that and had a celebratory beer on the tailgate. It was a fine afternoon and the highway was waiting and I had the whitefish to thank for being my first fish of the year. That's a pretty big deal when you think about it. I laid back in my truck bed and stared up at the clouds and that's when God started talking again. I started listening again. Kids have shitty lives and people think they know everything and lodges burn down and spring arrives late. Yet the sky can still be blue. The terns and the Harlequins can still exist. Some questions can stay unanswered and that can be okay. Some fish can be unsung.

I get back in the driver's seat and pull back onto the road. God save the whitefish, I think, for someone else to enjoy, for someone else to toil over, for someone else to behold and be surprised by. First fish of the year.

God save 'em all.

THE MIRACLE OF FISH

I AM CONTINUALLY AMAZED THAT WE CAN CATCH FISH on a fly at all. Think about it. First and foremost, you and the fish have to be in the same location at the same time. This is no simple feat, and one that presupposes that not only did *you* make it there in the first place—a condition of such factors as time off of work, means of transport, performance of said transport, general bodily health, weather, road conditions, etcetera—but that the fish did, too. They had to make it past obstacles of their own.

Beyond that, there are all kinds of variables that must proceed to fit within a narrow range—that is, the range of success. The fish must be in the mood to take a fly, and then you have to present that fly in a way that's just so, and then the fish has to commit, and then you have to rise above your own pedigree of human stupidity long enough to land the thing. In practice, we know, it can be childishly simple (bluegills and bobbers, come on), but in theory, it can be as complicated as the physics of aviation.

When all of these factors happen to swirl to a confluence, and the variables somehow line up, the whole thing has, as Jeremy

Wade once said, "an element of magic to it." You get the feeling that something special has just happened. And when the quarry is anadromous like a king salmon or a steelhead (and therefore both seasonal *and* elusive), this something special borders on true religious experience. You're testing a series of odds that just get longer and longer as they compound upon one another. You're wandering the improbable.

In this sense, it's no wonder that fly fishing is often the impetus for the larger philosophical questions of mankind:

What does it mean to be happy? Usually having a fly rod in your hand.

Why are anadromous fish so agreeable one day and hopelessly elusive the next? That's just the way it is.

And what the hell are all those Bob Dylan songs about? No idea.

My own impetus for this kind of deep thinking, as it often goes, was a text from my buddy Andy that came in early June. John and I are headed south for kings next weekend, it went. Care to join?

It's a good thing I didn't pause to calculate the long odds of this particular quest before I agreed to it. I was fresh off of a fruitless steelhead binge that left me haggard and cynical, and though catching a king salmon on a fly had been on my priority list for a while, I wasn't exactly betting the farm on my chances. Luckily I had a moment of clarity, though: if all you ever go fishing for are good odds, you might as well sell the rod collection and play the stock market instead. Or sell insurance. Who cares at that point?

I had a few things on my mind that could do with some ventilation, and anyway, I figured my chances of hooking a king with Andy were about as good as they would get. To use his own turn-of-phrase, Andy is one 'fishy' dude, and I hoped at least some of it would wear off on me. The other thing about Andy is that he attracts devoted fish gurus as though he's flypaper, so I could only assume that John—whom I'd never met—was 'fishy' as well. He couldn't be all that bad seeing as how he offered to drive.

THERE I WAS SITTING IN JOHN'S RV AS IT RUMBLED south on Alaska's Sterling Highway, feeling every tiny ripple in the asphalt as my bladder screamed in agony. This is where the trip started for me. We'd stopped in Soldotna for pizza, but all I knew was that there on the road, something like an hour later, I had to pee worse than I ever had in my life. That's a special thing, you know, to *know* something is the worst it's ever been for you. There were several beers and a good dose of water down there rioting against the fire exit, and finally it got so bad that I had to ask John to stop the RV because Dear Lord things were about to get catastrophic. Everything was fine after that.

The campground we were staying at was alive with the uncontained and unabashed bustle of a limited-time offer: salmon season. Word was that the kings were trickling in with the sockeyes close behind, and the resulting crowds looking to bonk these fish were composed of more people than the Wyoming town I grew up in.

Andy, John, and I weren't worried. We had a plan. We'd leave the bright afternoon fishing to the masses and return when the sun had lowered and the kings were (theoretically) more likely to attack a fly.

By the time we got on the water, it was nearing ten o'clock. Throngs of fishermen passed in the opposite direction on the trail, some looking dazed and disappointedly empty-handed, others empty-handed but tottering cheerily under the influence of a local pilsner. John was still back at the RV gearing up, but Andy and I located a long open section of water to fish and positioned ourselves appropriately.

The prevailing tactic around us was something known as the 'Kenai flip'. Basically, without any casting whatsoever, the angler continually 'flips' a predetermined amount of line equipped with enough weight to tick along the bottom and a buoyant-enough fly to hover at approximately fish level. It's glorified snagging. Lest

I sound holier-than-thou, let me point out that this is often the only way to catch sockeye salmon, and a method I employ happily when I'm of a harvest mindset. Flipping for *king salmon*, though—as many of these folks were doing—is on an order not far below heresy. It's about as bad as dipnetting for cohos.

Andy and I were purists of the swung fly, thank you very much, so we stood there for a while doting upon our sink-tips and articulated patterns of marabou, ostrich, and bunny. Andy had brought his "B-Team" fly box, meaning an assortment of flash flies and bunny streamers in the right colors for kings, but a little on the small side. I, on the other hand, went for the ostentatious principle: big and bright to the point they were nearly absurd.

We proceeded to fish.

With each cast, the worries that had lined up in my brain dulled. So what if it was June and I still didn't have a teaching job for the impending school year? I was standing in a river with a new eight-weight in hand paying out the slow glide of fly line. And that novel I'd spent the last two years writing and rewriting, so what if it had finally been rejected by the only two literary agents who gave it the time of day? Screw 'em.

I wish I had more of a build-up for you, a sort of narrative crescendo in which the lowly fisherman struggles through these disappointments until finally stumbling upon that euphoric miracle of a king salmon—but I don't. I made perhaps ten casts and, what do you know, one of those times the line jiggled as though a cat was batting the other end and I came tight to something big. I managed to croak out to Andy, who waddled bankward to retrieve the net only to discover that there was no net because there was still no John. We could only suspect that he'd found something intriguing in the beer cooler. Meanwhile I stood there attached to what felt like a rodeo bull, a mixture of Cloud Nine and pure fear steadily increasing the tremor in my knees.

King salmon are a fish that command respect, and not just when they're ripping line and bulldogging into glacial silt with the attitude of a Sherman tank. It's hard not to be envious of a fish that does what the salmon does. They hatch, they swim to the ocean, they swirl around there for a while, and then they return to freshwater in one heroic journey and make the ultimate sacrifice at the end of it all. If this were a person's life story, they'd have a Purple Heart and a biopic from Paramount. It's been estimated that only one or two salmon in every three thousand complete their entire life cycle from hatching to spawning. Every salmon that I could possibly encounter here, especially the one on the end of my line, was quite literally a miracle; living, pulsating proof that all of a thousand long odds which include brown bears, orcas, and gillnets can, in fact, be duped every now and then.

By the time the fish and I were wearing out, another group of fishermen had sidled over to enjoy the spectacle. Andy was able to borrow their net and aptly swooped my prize; a twenty-five-pound Chinook hen as bright as an engagement ring. I stood there gawking at her like a toad.

Moments later, I killed that fish with a couple of poorly-placed strikes with a rock. Even though she was a hatchery specimen, I still felt parasitic guilt as she lay there stiffened, eyes bulging like, well, a dead fish. *Did I have to*? No. *Why did I*? I don't know; maybe because when in Rome you do as the Romans do. Maybe because I'm a carnivore through and through, and because I was relying on the same type of gut instinct that brought the salmon here to spawn in the first place.

I've often considered the paradox of catch-and-release fishing, and moreover fishing itself. I do it again while scything a borrowed fillet knife down the salmon's spine. In seeking to protect vast areas of the American West, early conservationists assigned the land (and its inhabitants) an intrinsic value. This value had nothing to do with what people could stand to gain from the natural resources; it quantified the satisfaction of just knowing they were there. You could sit at a desk in New Jersey and be fulfilled by the thought of bighorn sheep roaming freely two thousand miles away in the same way that, say, a logger would be fulfilled by a barge of stripped timber floating downriver. Shouldn't we, then, be able to assign intrinsic value to sportfish, to the thought that somewhere out there, all those wondrous salmon and steelhead are existing, fighting their way to the next generation and, in a way, immortality? Shouldn't that be enough for people who profess to love these silver rogues?

The problem, of course, is that it's not. It's not enough to consider and to love an idea of a fish. I have to see it; I have to *hold* it and watch the intrinsic value turn to beauty in my hands, like stone turned to gold. That's my curse of being human.

Back at the camper, I shoved my gutted salmon into a mini freezer and had to brace my feet against the opposite wall to close the door. John, Andy, and I sat in the dimness. It was midnight.

I found John to be a pleasant fellow. This is a guy who breathes fly fishing and has spent time chasing taimen in Mongolia, sheefish on the Kobuk, and golden dorado in Uruguay, among other things and other places. He's quiet like me (unless he has something to say, in which case it's usually profound or hilarious), and his casting is slick and precise, like the movements of a heron.

John is somewhere in his fifties, so it only made sense for Andy (who is in his forties) to razz him about being gray, stiff, and stuck on cultural references that had long since decayed into the Earth. John's response was always good-natured, if somewhat poignant. "Growing old is like frying bacon in the nude," he'd say. "You know it's gonna hurt, you just don't know where."

It didn't take long for the both of them to turn on me.

"How old are you, Joe—like seven?"

"Does your mom know you're out this late?"

"Do you even know who that is on the radio?"

Of course I knew. It was Bob Dylan, though I had no idea what he was singing about and neither did John or Andy. John started isolating some of the lyrics and analyzing them within his coffers of memory, but the best he could do was tell me that "Hurricane" was about a boxer and that I should Google the other ones. (Andy was impressed he knew what Google was).

By then it was three a.m. I swear I could feel my brain deteriorating inside my skull, the neurons clasping for the memory of my king salmon; what she felt like, what she *really* felt like. I've since decided that trying to wrangle these memories is like trying to catch smoke. You'll never really remember because the event was fleeting, like the passage of a meteor, and now it's gone. All I want to do is crawl inside my sleeping bag and fall off the face of the Earth for a while. But I can't do that. There's more fishing to be had.

Andy and I tackle round two; John nurses a sore shoulder. We fish in the sterling predawn and watch as an armada of guide boats drift downriver, some dropping anchors and easing into soft water, others paddling hard to get ahead of the others. We catch nothing and return to the campground, fingers smarting with cold. John is snoring when we arrive, and since he's the only one who knows how to activate the third pullout bed, I'm left to set up my tent in the gravel. Andy offers his sympathies and closes the camper door.

I DON'T REMEMBER WHEN I WOKE UP, but I think it was sometime around ten in the morning. Pulling an all-nighter for king salmon is one of the few occasions where sleeping that late is acceptable.

I blunder out into a blinding sun to find Andy, similarly bedraggled, watching a group of eastern Europeans smoke cigarettes and toil over a lawn chair. This is the classic "smoke 'em if you got 'em" situation, but since neither Andy nor I have the habit, we bum around prodding through our fly boxes. We won't fish again until the evening, which leaves a great big void of in-between. I can't even call it preparation, really. Everything we need is all ready to go at a moment's notice; waders dried over the camper's side mirrors, rods strung up and leaning against the windshield. It's more a matter of waiting for the swarms of weekenders to leave and for the sun to tug us over into the shadow world of king salmon. I make several treks down to the river to see how the fishing is. Some people are catching sockeyes, others are duking it out with the occasional king (you can tell the difference by the pitch of the anglers' whoops). Most of these fish have come from the flipping technique, and I can't deny that I feel a smug sense of elevation having caught mine with more refined techniques.

Around dinnertime Andy, John, and I agree on the prudence of one more nap before showtime. We're maximizing our chances—stacking the odds—by fishing late; now we've just got to recharge enough to capitalize on them. I close my eyes and stare up at the inside of my tent. Bright orange, bright like the sun bouncing back off of water. It's not sleep that bags me. It's something better. It's that memory that once thundered away like an asteroid but now—*now*—it slows within some gravitational perigee and I catch it.

I'm there the night before, that magical night that went something like this:

The sun is low. It's where it's supposed to be to make you know it's time. You can taste the dusk like chalk on your teeth. A crepuscular world is stirring, the dark is stirring, and though it happens every day, it's a miracle. You've jumped all those obstacles; the fish have, too. Now you're here.

There's an eagle on the far bank, wasting time. Watch him. Feel a million years' worth of river soldiering by as your fly line cuts a small, a young, an improbable piece of it. Don't think about the teaching job you don't have. Don't think about all those mornings you've spent writing a novel that no one wants. Don't think. Just be.

Just be and hold on to that because in the instant that it takes the light of a shooting star to reach you, in the instant that this same light will burn out, something reaches out and grabs you. A salmon. Life in its purest form. Never mind that none of it makes sense, that the variables somehow lined up despite astronomical odds, or that happiness won't come from this moment until later because right now all you are is instinct. Hold on. Step downstream. Feel.

You'll forget a lot of things. But not this. Even when you think it's gone, it's in your spine safe and sound. It was there when you were an embryo, and it'll be there when you're not. The instinct, the swing of chrome to vermillion, ocean to stream; the miracle.

Feel the cork thrum.

Listen to the salmon sing its magnum opus. Listen to the sound as it fades into recollection, as it fades into the dark of the camper where you sit waiting. Next to you, Andy is gazing out into the gloom with a flicker of hope in his eyes, and John is puzzling over the radio and just what in the hell Bob Dylan was singing about all those years ago.

I snap myself out of it as I hear graphite tap against the windshield. Andy and John have taken up their rods.

It's time.

FOSSILS AND THE FOURTH OF JULY

THE SUPREME PEST OF THE EARTH IS NOT the mosquito. It's not even COVID-19. It's those people who park their campers in gravel pits for the Fourth of July.

There they are, huge hulking fifth-wheels with more square footage than a Manhattan condo. They bear names like the *Impact* or the *Momentum* or the *Vibe*, and almost always, they're parked haphazardly as though their owner meant to straighten them out but got distracted instead. Their ubiquity in Alaska is startling; once the snow melts, they seem to spawn out of thin air.

Roadside gravel pits are common in Alaska, too. Most of them are relics of the highway building days when bedrocks were excavated by the ton and packed under the asphalt to tame the permafrost and the muskeg. Some of the pits have been recolonized by shrubbery; others remain sterile thanks to the constant battering of tires and snowmachine tracks.

The big gravel pits get busy in the summer. I'm talking busy like the State Fair gets busy. There's one pit, in particular, not far from Eureka, that would probably become Alaska's biggest city if anyone cared to take a census there over Fourth of July weekend. It's a sweeping, reasonably level patch of ground, perhaps five acres or so, right off the highway with no parking fees and a view of the mountains. What's not to like? The place attracts recreational motherships—the Impacts and the Momentums and the Vibes—like glucose draws ants. What's ironic to me is that most of them come out to escape the city, but instead just create another version. The soundscape becomes less the constant groan of commuters and faint shouting of homeless people and more the constant buzz of two-stroke engines and the drunken epiphanies of the family parked fifteen feet away. When you think about all of the trash and nonsense they bring (and carelessly discard) to quaint Alaska, it can really simmer the blood.

As it is, though, these campers don't affect me much, even though I might pretend they do. The worst that can happen is getting stuck behind a motorcade of these gravel-bound buckaroos and having to make a sketchy pass on the two-lane. That's essentially how it started for me on an evening in early July. I left our apartment in Anchorage at eleven o'clock p.m. and planned to fish a certain river in the Copper Valley as soon as I arrived, roughly two or three in the morning. I'd be running completely on caffeine and Metallica, but I'd live. And maybe catch a sockeye.

Driving that late and that far always makes me feel delinquent. Like I'm on a mission that nobody understands. Maybe I don't even understand. I just know that salmon season comes and goes so you'd better make the best of it. Suffer the consequences later if there are any.

Alaska at midnight is a special place. It's not like Alaska the rest of the time. Somehow it's prettier and friendlier. The low light makes everything feel attainable, as though you could hike that mountain peak ten miles distant, or drive to Fairbanks and back before breakfast, or have half a chance at hooking one of the invisible anadromous migrants swimming just feet from your boots. Whatever you want, it can happen. What an intoxicating illusion.

It felt like I took the drive slow that night but I didn't at all. I rollicked around the curves and smashed the gas pedal on straightaways. I needled past motorhomes and tow-behinds and stopped only once to pee in, get this, a gravel pit. I usually stop at one in particular because it's roughly halfway through the drive to the Copper Valley, and because it's got a neat story:

This is where one of Alaska's most complete dinosaur skeletons was found. I like to stand there and think about that while I let 'er fly.

The Glenn Highway started in the '30s by connecting Anchorage to the agricultural community of Palmer. During World War II, it came to be expanded; Alaska proved not only a good locale from which to ship weapons to the Soviet Union, but a highly likely candidate for a catastrophic Japanese invasion. A network of military-grade highways were proposed and built to connect the Far North to the continental United States and solve both problems. There's really nothing like war—or the threat of it—to kick construction projects into high gear. The Glenn was completed as part of this effort in 1945, along with the 1,420-mile monstrosity of the Alcan Highway. Alaska was suddenly connected to the rest of the continent. It was nearly half a century later that our dinosaur story began.

It's September of 1994. There aren't so many motorhomes in the world yet. A woman by the name of Virginia May is stooped over some rocks just north of the Glenn Highway, presumably wielding a hammer and a chisel and maybe a horsehair brush. Various invertebrate fossils from the Jurassic and Cretaceous Periods have been found here before; this part of the Talkeetna Mountains, once a series of island arcs cast into an ocean ninety-million years ago, is now a cornucopia of prehistoric marine and terrestrial life. That's probably why our friend Virginia is here. But what she discovers next is not an invertebrate. It's not a cephalopod and it's not a protist and it's not an ichnofossil.

It's a hadrosaur, a duck-billed herbivore that wandered the food chains of the late Cretaceous. Think prehistoric camel and you've got the idea. (Some paleontologists prefer to compare hadrosaurs to today's beef cattle or white-tailed deer; endlessly abundant, endlessly effective at vacuuming the plant life from their vicinities.)

For all of their purported abundance, though, Virginia May's hadrosaur is one of the first of its kind. It *is* the first from this part of the state, and after some careful excavation, it turns out to be the most complete collection of a hadrosaur skeleton found anywhere in Alaska. By the summer of 1996, after hours and days and weeks of exhaustive excavation, the skeleton generated a bit of publicity. Over sixty bones and fragments had been found from what was determined to be a juvenile hadrosaur roughly ten feet long. Alaskan paleontologist Kevin May dubs the skeleton—and the animal it came from—"Lizzie," after his twelve-year-old daughter. Further research suggests that Lizzie is one of the earliest known hadrosaurs from anywhere in the world.

Not a bad story for a gravel pit, huh? I stand there and look at it and imagine what else could be down there. Paleontologists have uncovered loads of cool relics from these mountains. The first Alaskan *Elasmosaurus* (think thirty-foot-long Loch Ness monster) was pulled from a sixty-foot cliff in 2015, while a burly Ankylosaur called *Edmontonia* (nicknamed the "Talkeetna Tank") was found just before Lizzie was.

Despite several private property signs, a couple of campers occupy Lizzie's quarry when I stop. Canopy tents pulled out and trailers packed with four-wheelers. Their owners have absolutely no idea what happened here.

AT THIS POINT, I HAVE TO ADMIT THAT I DRAW significant amusement from Alaska's plague of campers and motorhomes. Sure, they aggravate the bejesus out of me on the average, but under the right circumstances they can usher tears of laughter. It's all part of an elaborate joke system. I did not invent it and I won't mention who did. They deserve the credit but not the blame. Here's how it works:

Whenever you see a camper or RV or motorhome on the road (more than likely because you're stuck behind it), or sprawled out in a gravel pit on the days leading up to the Fourth of July, you simply add the word *anal* to whatever its name may be. So if I pass a fifth-wheel dubbed the "Hideout," say, I'd have an "Anal Hideout." It's unabashed schoolboy humor, but it gets the job done. Interpretation is up to you.

Most campers are good for a chuckle or two. The Cougar, for example. Classic. Or the Impact. Some of them, like the Extra-Lite or the Fun Finder, could be titles to salacious Craigslist postings. Others serve to disturb more than to entertain: I don't like to think too deeply (you'll have to excuse the pun) about the Torque or the Voltage, nor do I especially like to dwell on the gastrointestinal-crises of the Hurricane or the Cyclone. All things considered, I think if camper companies knew the level of entertainment I get at the expense of their customers, they might not choose names like the Vibe or the Momentum or—and I'm not kidding, I saw this one once—the Assault.

Thoroughly satisfied that Emmie and I don't own a camper and are therefore immune to this brand of hoodlum hilarity, I arrived at my intended river at three in the morning. I'd had the good sense to rig up the rods at home four hours before, so I simply pulled them out of the truck and tootled down to my fishing spot.

When I say "my fishing spot," I really do mean it. It's about the size of a motorhome, incidentally, and in the eight years that I've been fishing it I like to think I've got it dialed. Devoted roadside anglers think it's too close to the bridge to be worth anything, and lazy roadside anglers think it's too far. It's also a natural pinchpoint in the fishery, forcing migrating sockeyes to slow down in a distinctive seam between the rushing main current and the slackened shoreside one. I can tell you exactly how many ounces of weight to use here, how many inches of fluorocarbon your leader needs to be, how much egg yarn and marabou to tie into your fly to achieve the correct buoyancy, how many feet to cast and at what angle to do it, and approximately where in the subsequent drift you're likely to hook a fish. This is not a reflection of my prowess as an angler (it's debatable whether I have any), but rather an indication of how much time I've spent there.

There's one other fisherman out there in the gloaming when I arrive. Straight across the river. Fishing as though in a hurry and hauling out a boom box. He spends a moment presumably hooking his phone up via Bluetooth.

I fish carefully in the faint thrumming of his music, accepting only perfect casts and noting how hard my rig is striking the riverbed. You want it just hovering over the bottom. Fish level. I snip the weight back a little and find a rock upon which to stand, to mark exactly where the drift must begin, and I make cast after cast into the marching currents.

A half hour later, the boom box guy has given up hope and surrendered, withdrawn, retreated from view. I've snagged the bottom a few times and either straightened my hooks or exhumed a snarled rig from yesteryear; hooks rusted into oblivion, lead weights worn soap-smooth. Most of these once belonged to other anglers. I can tell, whether from their outsized hooks, the absurd thickness of their monofilament, or the hastiness of their knots. Sometimes I wonder if my old rigs are entombed there, too. Eight years of fishing here so you know they've gotta be down there. Maybe tangled up so tight beneath boulders they'll never be found, maybe straggling in the current like living things.

If I could get to them, these old rigs would show an evolution of my efforts on this river. A fossil record. Varying leader lengths would reflect the rise and fall of water levels. Same with the weights. The flies will have lost their once-vibrant color but the pattern of materials will show unnecessary complexity at first, then a gradual adoption of minimalism. And finally the knots. These will show competence. Experience. The knots will show time.

At last I hook something solid that fights back. Four a.m., perhaps, the chalky taste of protein bars and mosquito repellent, the startled squeak of the reel, the line taut as a banjo string and strumming in sync with the wild horse-pulls of a fish. Sockeye salmon in this place are a little like love. You can't describe the feeling of hooking one, you'd never be able to, but you know it when it comes.

I land the fish and kill it and string it up in the shallows to cool and bleed out. I do it all with workday efficiency and then I get back to fishing. I'm dog-tired but I plant my feet and make the casts. Like I'm a machine. Like I can sleep standing up.

IT'S A RARE THING TO BECOME A FOSSIL. An astronomically rare thing, it turns out.

I think about that as I drive to my in-laws' farm. Six a.m. now. Success thumping around in the cooler; two buck sockeyes. My eyes itch and plead to close.

Scientists estimate that something like one percent of one-tenth of all animal species go on to become fossilized. Bill Bryson, in his groundbreaking *A Short History of Nearly Everything* from 2003, puts the figure at one in a billion bones (not animals—*bones*). The odds are stupid. I'll never become a fossil. You won't, either.

Fossilization requires a strict set of conditions. First, of course, you have to expire. But you must expire in a way that maintains as much of your anatomical integrity as possible. I suppose a heart attack would be ideal. Or just passing quietly in a fishing-induced sleep. Next, you have to be buried quickly. Quickly enough to be out of reach of scavengers and the elements, and quickly enough to be entombed both physically and chemically in a layer of sediment well-below ground level. It's best to do this in an area of low elevation, stagnant water, and low oxygen levels. Coastal river deltas are particularly good, which is why eastern Montana is such a hotbed for dinosaur research. The area was once a vast braided network of rivers draining into an inland sea.

That all sounds very academic until you actually calculate the odds themselves. What are the chances, for instance, that a sockeye salmon in this part of the world will be dug up by paleontologists a million years on? I've got nothing but time.

The average sockeye has around two hundred and sixty bones. Two hundred and sixty bones multiplied by the average Copper River sockeye run size (roughly 750,000) gets us right at one hundred and ninety-five million. So, in a typical year, one hundred and ninety-five million sockeye bones are noodling into this region as candidates for fossilization. If we go with Bill Bryson's posited figure (and I think we should—he's a smart dude), we'd need to divide one billion by one hundred and ninety-five million to determine how many years' worth of salmon runs it would take to have a shot at fossil-hood. The answer turns out to be just over five years.

That means that every half-decade, just *one* sockeye salmon bone is preserved in the fossil record. By that measure it'd take thirteen-hundred years before you'd get all the bones for a complete skeleton. And remember: neither answer says anything about the odds of those fossils being found. It makes you think hard about just what an odds-defying specimen Lizzie the hadrosaur was, and just how likely it is that everything you are and know and will ever be will simply be forgotten. All those hours you spent fishing for sockeyes. The swarms of campers and motorhomes with their coddled occupants and lewd nicknames. All of it forgotten, zapped, effaced. At least, in a geological sense.

I WAKE UP BLINKING LIKE AN OWL a few hours later. It's July 3rd. Has been for a while. Dates and times don't really register when your boots are in the river. I spend the afternoon piddling around and tying more sockeye flies. Red marabou, orange marabou, black marabou. A tuft of egg yarn. I don't think color matters, but confidence does.

At dinner I make various pitches to Emmie's family, trying to convince just one of them—my brother-in-law, Alex; my other brother-in-law Chris; my eight-year-old nephew, Vince; Emmie herself—to join me in the morning. 'Morning,' of course, means a two a.m. wakeup call. Nobody bites.

I'm awake in the lonely gloom just a few hours later, tugging on stiff jeans, stepping into the cold. Midnight Alaska makes everything brilliant, as though I can reach out and grab the Wrangell Mountains with their enameled glacier shells and their dusty shadows. Reach up and grab the stars, even, or at least the ones I can see. At the river I fish and don't even realize it's turned over to the Fourth of July. Don't know why I would. The days of the week are named after the Sun and the Moon and a handful of Norse gods. Independence Day was conjured by man. Salmon have got nothing to do with it. At one time they defined the days and the seasons; at one time it was their land and their rivers cut it all into pieces.

The fishing turns out to be spectacular. The best I've ever had on this river, in fact. It's as I'm clonking my second fish that the first squeal of fireworks creeps through the trees. I imagine them bursting way up there even though I can't see them. No one can. Fireworks have never worked on Alaska's Fourth of July. People still try, though.

They try to open up the sky and make it theirs. We are the best in the animal kingdom at altering our environment. Fireworks. Highways. Wi-Fi and music-on-demand and boom boxes you can haul down to the river, because God forbid you fish in silence; in the sound of the river and the gulls and the living throb of all that came before and what'll pass afterward. People flood out of the city and into the gravel pits as though in pilgrimage. Not so much to feel new winds as to block them with aluminum and glass, to be out there but only in a controlled way, a world within a world. To ignite careful measures of gunpowder in the name of freedom, or maybe in no name that they can remember.

I continue casting. The only way to ruin a morning of sockeye fishing is a quick limit. I'll hook other fish and release them. They'll swim from my fingers back into the imagined, this momentary reward from Midnight Alaska gone and done. The fish will spawn and die and rot or maybe the billion stars of probability will align and they'll be entombed in the records of the world and someone will find them someday and ask questions about them. I hope so, because right now people don't wonder enough.

I finally call it a morning when I hook the riverbed and manage to crank out a tangle of line. Old rigs, a whole snarl of them. Weathered and yellowed and ragged but still there. It'll take a couple hundred thousand years before you could call them a fossil, but somehow they feel old enough now. I untangle them and put the miscellaneous bits of line and rubber and lead into a trash bag, and in the mess I find one of my old rigs.

I know it by its signature of knots. Mine. Palomar-Palomar-double cinch. Who knows how many years old, but at least a couple. Perhaps all the way back to the birth of my obsession with this place. The first stage in a process, an archetype from which all subsequent versions stem. Taken together, maybe the rigs throughout the years display a formula; for sockeyes, for the Fourth of July. For all of the highway miles and delinquent wee hours that flowed in between. That's not a bad thought.

Maybe they craft a mosaic of the ephemeral—the place, the time, the potent sprigs of feeling that come back and return, year after year. Like sockeyes. Like campers, too, I guess, now that I think about it.

FIBERGLASS DAYDREAM

I'M SITTING THERE LISTENING TO A virtual training about virtual teaching, which is somehow even less interesting than it sounds. Somebody named Wanda expects us—a Zoom-room full of teachers with even shorter attention spans than our students—to follow along with a two-hour video and come away with a working knowledge of some-or-another learning management system. Yeah, right. It takes approximately seven seconds for my mind to wander.

A few years ago, I used most of my surplus funds (with a nice injection from Christmas and birthday money, which apparently people still feel sorry enough to give me) to buy my very first fiberglass rod. I had no idea about rod tapers or parabolic actions or anything of that sort; all I knew was that I wanted a devoted Alaskan grayling rod that was soft, could cast short leaders, and did justice to a lovely fish that's not known to be scrappy, but can be. My grandpa, Pops, fishes with a fiberglass of the spinning variety, and it's entirely possible that this old rod was the first one I ever held. Maybe it's the weight of that thought—maybe it's just my imagination—but my own fiberglass feels nostalgically familiar, as though an imprint of my thumb was already worn into the cork despite the rod being brand-new.

So here's the daydream: forget that Wanda is droning on and on about managing the gradebook. Forget that you'd like nothing more than to click that red button. You're on an unnamed stream in Alaska's Fortymile River valley.

Once a mecca for gold seekers even before the Klondike, this region is now home to copious amounts of gravel dust, the occasional historical interpretive sign, and as wild a population of grayling as can be found, if you care to look for them. (Which, of course, you do).

This is the place where that new fiberglass—before you snap its tip section in the rear window of your truck—shines. Take a knee in the cobbles. You could jump over the creek as it purls by, so you only need a false cast or two to lay it out there. "Let the rod do the work," your first casting instructor said. Heed his words. Let the fiberglass assume the shape of willows in a breeze. Drop it. The tub where the old grayling sits is smaller than a kitchen sink.

The fly is one you tied yourself with orange thread and snowshoe hare's foot. You even hunted the white rogues yourself, stomping through twenty-below back in January with a snappy little rimfire in your mitts. It's amazing how their white fur just disappears in the snow; it's amazing now how quickly it vanishes in the grayling's rise.

Water here is both restless and patient. You realize that fiberglass is the same. To that end, it's kind of like *you*: practically bursting with latent energy but just old enough to be patient about using it. The line that connects to grayling connects to this faux-philosophy, too, and even though it might be nonsense, somehow it sounds right in your head. Back in the '40s, you think, fly rod companies first started to make their sticks out of fiberglass rather than the split-cane standard. Cheaper material made for cheaper rods. Accessible, expendable, even then defined as "whippy." The prime of 'glass lasted until the '70s when graphite and boron emerged and people realized you could hit seventy-foot casts without being Joan Wulff. You start to think that you may have just caught the beginning of some fiberglass revival wave, a period in which millennials get sentimental and want to fish something softer and more contemplative—like their grandpa used, for example. It's kind of like cars; you'll have those genuinely ancient folks longing for "how they used to make 'em," with their voices invariably echoed by a caste of younger squirts who crave some classic that their generation was deprived of.

Just like they don't make 'em like they used to, in most places the fishing ain't as good as it used to be. Not here. That's evidenced by the fact that you've seen exactly one other fisherman in just over two hundred miles of road. People are fishing bigger water for bigger fish elsewhere, and likely with graphite. You look down at the grayling in your net, sequined in sky-blue, honey-gold, silver as pure as Spanish doubloons. All fish are exponentially prettier in the water than out, but this is especially true of the Arctic grayling. They're not made to be removed, so you don't. You let him vanish from the world and you move upstream, savoring an atomic sun and the fact that, as far as you and your hip boots are concerned, this creek goes on forever.

It's only then that you start to realize that your feet aren't planted in gravel, but on an ergonomic rubber mat resting on a hardwood floor. The air isn't so effortlessly clean that it smells of spruce resin, but it isn't bad thanks to the air purifier in the hallway.

Your fiberglass rod—both classic and new—was repaired right at the end of last season. It's sitting in a silver tube in the closet and you think a few casts in the yard this afternoon may not be out of line, even with two feet of snow on the ground. Then you snap back because you realize that Wanda is no longer talking, and you figure out that Wanda is no longer talking because you're the only one left.

Meeting's over.

DIE TO LIVE

TWO A.M. AND I'M UP IN THE DARK of a one-bedroom apartment, pawing for a pair of socks and the six-weight behind the door. Don't wake the wife. Outside it's the hour when the neighbor's dog finally shuts up and the crackheads go to sleep. The hour of frost on the windshield. Aurora in the sky. You'd better believe I packed everything last night (save for the rod), so I pull away fifteen minutes ahead of schedule. Fatigue and angst and sanity pull at me from every direction. What's there to do but drown it out with the chords of a metal band.

One hour. Two. Coffee down the hatch, pee on the asphalt. Lynx on the shoulders crouching low as if I can't see them. A hitchhiker, grim, with his face into the wind.

I pass like a needle through the Alaska Range, feeling puny but godlike all at once. The tourist mecca of Denali Village, though aglow with hotel chandeliers and the only stoplight for two hundred miles during the summer, is dead as the apocalypse now. Windows boarded up, tourists gone even though this is the best time of the year. I grin at their loss and stomp the pedal harder.

I'm awake in this lonely trout mission. Awake in all it can make me forget. I'm heading home, to the place where hearts are broken, to where my pulse quickens because it has to, to the creek where you know full-well that the sign saying "No Overnight Camping" means instead, "Enter at your own risk." To the gilded beauty of a place I die to live.

Now there are brake lights in the distance like insect eyes. A potential competitor, someone to beat me to the stream, so I coax the gas and moments later I pass them. They charge me more for insurance because I'm young. Might as well drive fast.

Cantwell comes sooner than it should, even though I know better—that's where the troopers always sit—and I slam on the brakes just a few miles out not for the sake of avoiding a ticket but to check on the water of the East Fork. It's clear but low, the vestiges of a summer haunted by drought and wildfires; conditions in which trout can watch egg flies drift by and make a bulleted list of why they didn't come from a real salmon. Wrong color. Wrong shape. *Don't eat those, boy,* their granddad probably said once. *Don't eat those eggs that look funny.* Advice that passed through the grapevine to every trout in town. I climb back up to the truck, morning and foliage and salmon flesh rotting in the air.

There's onward to go. The sky is still black as Gargantua and stars poke through it like they're trying to be noticed. Doesn't matter if I look at them or not; they all string together in constellations shaped like trout.

An hour or two later I'm there. First one. Ryan's Creek. No one else is dumb enough to wait an hour in the dark.

I plunge into waders and listen to the murmurs of leaves, soaked with what little September rain there is, tumbling down to become vole fodder. I imagine the bears out there, big hulking shapes, gorgons with red eyes. Then I see myself here a month ago, when the sun was shining and the sky was blue, when the trout weren't educated yet and they struck with the reckless abandon of the young and dumb. I had just looked up from sight-fishing a little rogue trout to find two rogues of a different kind hugging a poplar twenty feet up. Grizzly cubs.

There's something electric—something *heavy metal*—about staring danger in the face like that, even if it's pretty cute and nascent from a spring birth. Of course I didn't waste time contemplating that. Of course I got the hell out of there. Mama had to be close.

"You're alright, guys," I crooned.

Please don't send your mother after me. Yes, I know she could show me what the inside of my skull looks like.

But seconds later I found her. Middle of the creek, quartered away. I froze.

An eagle burst from her carcass and the stench hit me. She'd been lying there for a while, ribcage picked clean by woody beaks, flesh bleached by the sun and shredded like the tattered hems of a bridal gown. Even though I stay on edge all day looking for her kind and I've known people to have been mauled within an inch of their life by her brethren, I decided that I'd rather have her alive than dead. Her cubs were far too small to make a go of it alone. I moved on, hating whoever it was that made them orphans, because you know it wasn't natural causes there in the middle of the water. I hated 'em the way you can hate monsters, the way you can hate the devil.

Now I blink and the memory decays. I'm back to staring out the windshield, awaiting the first glimpse of daylight. September. Vole fodder.

It comes faster than I think. Like it always does. Soon the dawn melts into silver day and it just becomes hour after hour. The fish are spooky as I suspect, but I manage one or two. Enough to never be enough, basically. That's what I tell people. I make a cup of coffee at the mouth of the creek and chug it so fast that I burn the back of my throat, then I eat half of my lunch and keep moving down a bank littered in bear tracks. Always keep moving, even if you're hungry. *Especially* if you're hungry. Fast like a moose in the rut.

Trout don't wait. Nothing does. You can eat later, hydrate later, die later. Not today.

I'm cold and dog-tired and cut up by alder branches on the hike back. I can already feel the hangover coming for me tomorrow, when I sleep in and wake up confused and my head splits and my body aches. Like I escaped war, somehow, like the hours I spent were actually years.

I can feel that trout hangover, you betcha, but I push it away for now. I salute the creek and exit my waders and change socks and make a fresh charge of coffee and wonder if the beavers will have the place dammed up next year. Back on the highway the hours go slow and the road goes a little too fast. My spine vibrates with the speakers and the rain I needed a month ago patters the windshield.

I'm only a half hour from home when I pass the trooper. Eighty-three in a sixty-five. I know I'm caught even before his lights explode.

"Any reason you're driving like a bat out of Hell?" he asks, a short while later as he sidles up to the window.

I hand over the sundries and try to conjure a look of guilt.

"Not a bat out of Hell," I want to say. "A rainbow that's just been hooked."

He shows no mercy and I go on home, trying to relive the takes and the leaps instead of the citation snarling at me from the dashboard. I pass the same hitchhiker that I saw that morning in the dark. He's still grim and he's still walking. He hasn't made it very far.

THE ROOSEVELT ROOSTER

I FIRST MET HIM IN SEPTEMBER OF 2021.
Emmie and I had been slated to go to Yakutat for a few days of coho fishing, but southeast Alaska got pummeled with rain and the rivers we'd planned to fish started flooding to biblical proportions. ('Biblical' here means ten times their normal flow and violent enough to drown two experienced watermen in a jet boat.) We canceled everything the day before we flew out.

Flooded creeks on my own turf put trout fishing out of the question, so I was stranded in the dangerous territory of a wasted weekend. I hadn't really felt the itch to grouse hunt much up until that point, but it seemed to be my antidote; a legitimate excuse (or thereabouts) to get out and make the most of a fleeting season. There was also an expanse of grouse woods not a half hour from our apartment that was practically endless as far as I was concerned, and it was entirely open to anyone patient enough to brave the red tape of entering a military fence. I set out with low expectations, no idea that a new obsession was about to grab me and shake me like a ragdoll.

You practically have to enlist to get onto the Army base for recreation. Maybe that's the scheme. You've gotta get an annual hunting permit, register any and all firearms you intend to bring past the gates right down to the serial number and barrel length, and check in at the visitor center for temporary credentials every time you go out. Thanks to all of that paperwork, the military knows exactly—which street address, which room, which closet—where my shotgun resides.

Still, this Army base demands some attention. It remains the only spot that I can conceivably hunt on a weeknight after school, or on a quick weekend morning when my original plans fall through. I'll deal with stone-faced bureaucracy for that. Plus it's always interesting to see some of the stuff the military leaves in the woods.

The first time I went out there I hunted a place called Snipe Lake. It's a popular spot with the military families in the summer, and as such it boasts an expansive campground. In late September it felt like an abandoned Six Flags. I picked the spot because, from the satellite maps, it looked like it contained a good mix of deciduous and coniferous trees. That's basically the extent of my grouse knowledge. I know they need the deciduous zones because these contain food (your high-bush cranberries and willow or aspen buds), and the evergreens make good year-round cover. There was a river cutting through some hills to the north of the lake, and I figured I could walk that way and hunt the riparian zones for a few hours. On maps, these types of plans are easy. In reality, I just wandered circles around the lake, trying not to think about all of the cartwheeling cohos I may have missed out on in Yakutat.

I flushed up two snipe right off the bat, which I didn't shoot at because at first I didn't know what they could be. Best not to get too trigger-happy with a fleet of F16s less than a mile away. The snipe is a curious little bird. You hear them all the time in the spring, usually in the early mornings when they go sprocketing across the sky belting a call that sounds like a cross between a boreal owl and an air-raid alarm. That day they proved to be harbingers of some rare success, because not ten minutes later I bagged a double of a cock and hen spruce grouse as they hammered over a gravel lane. I could count my lifetime grouse harvest on one hand at that point, so to bag two from one covey rise—well, you can imagine. Forget dignity; forget rational thought. It's not often you can point to a single instant as the start of something great, but I can: carrying those two grouse and my old Remington 870 back toward the truck, the air an imbibement, the leaves tap-dancing across the gravel, wishing I could breathe the moment forever. I knew nothing about bird hunting—still don't—except that I was head-over-heels for it.

I called it a day after that and headed home, riding the high of harvested birds and Tom Petty on the radio. I was functionally zoned out when a furious shape lifted off the road ahead of me and vanished into the trees. Grouse. I logged that bend in the gravel lane as a mental waypoint to return to later.

Many times later, as it would turn out.

IT WAS AN AFTERNOON AFTER SCHOOL LET OUT, the day old but the sunset young. I'd gotten onto the base in relatively good time, even despite the old fellow at the gate who signed me in with the efficiency of a porcupine. I followed the maze of roads that get less and less maintained the farther you go, passed a few platoons of fresh recruits marching in unpracticed sync, and then I parked at the entrance to an old two-track and plunged into the trees.

Had I not seen the bird here a week before, I'd have never come to explore this particular cover. There was absolutely nothing to distinguish it from any other patch of boreal; it was thorny, swampy, and dusky. Few shooting lanes for a novice. Lots of canopy for grouse to ghost you in. Some grunt laborers—perhaps the same I'd seen marching—had laid some barbed wire fence there not too long ago, but they hadn't planted any 'Unexploded Ordnance' signs so I crossed it and didn't think much of it. Ten steps and I kicked up an old fixed-wing drone. Thankfully it didn't obliterate me.

I hunted and tried not to tell myself that all I'd have was beginner's luck. That those two grouse I bagged the other weekend would be all I'd get; the only validation that, occasionally, a person could look for gamebirds and actually find them.

Slowly the forest got darker and heavier, and with each step my thoughts became less and less complex. Finally they settled on the distant hum of no thinking at all. Just reacting and feeling. Chickadees in the trees. The fast glimpse of a hare roiling away through the alders. Then, out of nowhere, the sudden, spine-rattling thump of a grouse cupping the air. Just a glimpse but I knew it was a male. Spruce grouse. Feathers thickened and battleship gray, tailfan spread wide like jet flaps, obsidian eyes calculating a flight path. It didn't occur to me until then to call a male grouse a rooster, but something about the fleeing shape in the sky demanded some form of dignification, the way a crowing at sunrise does. A rooster he became.

I ran into him again a few days later. Same story: left school after the bell rang, fetched the gun and the vest from the apartment, waited three thousand years while the old man at the gate endeavored to read my driver's license, then finally made it to the cover.

I hunted it the same way, followed in my same set of tracks in the mushy tannic earth. Let my thoughts drift into the shapeless. Then, in the exact same clump of white spruce where he'd exploded before, a zone no larger than a tennis court amidst acres of apparently viable country, that wily old spruce cock—excuse me, *rooster*—launched himself skyward with the noise of an old Hercules missile. He startled me to pieces and, as you'd expect, inaction. The gun came to my shoulder but far too late. He was gone.

THERE I WAS A YEAR LATER.

I had a few more birds to my name by that point—more spruce grouse in other places and a few high-country ptarmigan—and my knowledge of their habits had tilted from totally academic to knocking on the door of the practical. I even had a new gun, a tight little 20-gauge that made shots I know I can't take credit for. The sudden chaos of grouse-flight didn't stun me into wordless babble anymore so much as snap the gun to my shoulder, and I knew if ever there was a time that I was prepared enough to pay the rooster another visit, it was now. Maybe part of me knew I'd get duped again, but somewhere I knew I'd be okay with it. Everyone can do with some humility now and then.

It was a Sunday. Mostly indistinguishable from that Saturday that Emmie and I should've spent in Yakutat catching cohos a year previous—a loose plan to grouse hunt, a set of low expectations, a swelling sense of gratitude at having a place so close to home and a burgeoning addiction to something new. Here's how it went:

I park near the old two-track. I take my time vesting up and loading the gun. Win, lose, or draw, I want to savor the moment. Hold the air in my lungs as long as I can. The September afternoon. Around me the woods feel tired.

Guys hunt this place all the time with bows for moose, but I've never run into another grouse hunter. Now here in the rooster's cover, I'm alone again. You've gotta wonder if the bird's still alive or if he succumbed to the likelier odds of winterkill or great-horned owl strike. Maybe the forest is empty now; maybe his death would make this hallowed ground.

I'm twining myself through an alder thicket. The sound of a bird flushing is far and faint, so much that I write it off at first, but then I catch the sight of him again. Tail fan, cycling wings. Nobody's ever called a spruce grouse a rooster, just like nobody's ever called one 'The King.' But I do. Friend, nemesis. Rooster, king.

He's an old bird and he takes refuge in a thickened spruce, way up where he'd be invisible if I hadn't watched him land there. His scaled dinosaur feet fidget on the branch. He's gonna go at any moment. I find what could pass as a shooting lane and just as I step he goes, down toward the ground and his practiced escape. Out the back door. The gun comes to my shoulder and I throw a round out and just as he passes out of view there's a puff of feathers. Soft thud of a body in the moss.

I'm triumphant over nothing. Lucky, maybe. The saga of an old grouse—one that had duped not only me, but the long odds of his survival in a place where drones are abandoned and young men march—was over. Eons to a bird like him, a scribble to a man like me, all of it punctuated with a blast of seven-and-a-halfs as he cannonaded out of that tall spruce. The Army knows which closet I keep my shotgun in, but they'll never know what happened here.

I cleaned the rooster on a nearby riverbank later that evening. The sun had receded and the shadows were puddled up. A moose hunter rolled in, checking things out, hoping for a cow within range. He found me instead.

"Seen any moose?"

"Naw, grouse hunting."

He looked at the rooster in my hand and shifted the truck back into gear.

"Nice bird."

He wasn't wrong.

NEW GUN

My FIRST SIDE-BY-SIDE SHOTGUN WAS ALSO the first gun I ever bought myself. I ordered it on a Saturday in early August and it showed up four days later; for better or worse, the day before school started.

Its arrival ushered the same sort of behavior in a social studies teacher of twenty-six as it would have if I were a schoolboy of fourteen. I broke the gun out of its box at least twice a day before and after school just to gawk at it: its clean elegant lines, its case-hardened steel, its regal Turkish walnut polished soap-smooth. I'd put it together with the care of a lapidary, play with the action, throw it to my shoulder and track pigeons and chickadees out the back window. You know, pretend to fold them all.

I was lucky enough to be dropped into the childhood of most gun enthusiasts, by which I mean I had a father who was a gun enthusiast. Dad had an arms collection (still does) that, as far as I was concerned, was infinite. More importantly, he had a generous-enough heart to bequeath me with pieces of this collection about as soon as they became appropriate for my steadily growing age. At eight, it was a Rossi Model 62 rimfire, perfect for cottontails and squirrels and plinking up by the canal. At twelve it was a .270 for my first antelope hunt, at fourteen it was a Mossberg 20 gauge. Sixteen ushered in a Ruger Bearcat .22 pistol; eighteen a Remington Model 870 12 gauge as I headed off to Alaska for college. By twenty-six I figured I was old enough and employed enough to buy my own (although the first thing Dad did when I said I wanted a purist grouse gun was offer me his old SKB).

In selecting a side-by-side, there was the obvious "buy used" route to take. This would've included the purchase of some nostalgic weight; somebody's grandpa's gun, or what used to sit behind the mudroom door at Uncle Gene's house, that sort of thing. The other option was to buy new, though it would have to be of economic Turkish make as I didn't want to sell my truck to get my hands on one. I spent weeks pretending to research the various pros and cons of several models; in the end I just opted for what I felt was the prettiest.

The first time I shot it went about like I'd expected. At best I hit about seventy percent of the clays that got chucked within my line of fire, and at worst it was something like thirty. I'm a shoddy wingshooter even with some practice, but there in August on the verge of a wondrous grouse season, I'd not fired a scattergun since the previous October. But man was it a joy to shoot.

The buddy I was shooting with, Tim, who'd recently been transplanted from Iowa to Alaska and who nurtures similar affections for gamebirds, looked the gun up and down.

"At least you can miss with a pretty gun," he said.

THE MORNING OF SEPTEMBER THE FIRST was full of cold air. And rain. Lots of rain. The leaves had begun to drain of their succulent greens, geese were clamoring somewhere within the clouds and congregating in the soccer field at school, and my longing for grouse woods had turned as palpable as a sizzling powerline. Alaska's upland season technically opens August 10th, but it doesn't really feel appropriate until the calendar flips over to September.

I managed to get out on my first hunt of the year shortly thereafter. The rain had stopped but it was foggy as a witch coven. I'd picked a patch of open ground in the Copper River Valley because I'd heard rumors it harbored sharptails, but one step into the silvery muskeg suggested I'd endure a living hell trying to find them. Everything was soaked. I stuck to the gravel road instead, throwing the gun to my shoulder every now and then for kicks, not really expecting much besides an early morning walk with this new gun of mine.

It usually happens that when you set your expectations low like this—or avoid developing them altogether—they come to be exceeded. That's probably not true in a statistical sense, but maybe it's just that, since you expect things to play out so tepidly, anything that can be considered even a slight improvement seems disproportionately charming.

Out of the mists appeared a family of grouse picking grit from the road, and despite their flushing wild into the trees as soon as I took another step, I managed to follow them up through the woods and shoot one as he blasted away in the direction I least wanted him to take. His plump body thunked against the forest floor and I stood there like someone had just smacked me with a circus mallet.

My first bird with the new gun.

Into my vest it went, and not two steps later another gamey bird rattled overhead and the gun, as if on its own accord, jumped up to my shoulder and then against it with a bark as this grouse, too, tumbled to the moss.

Two birds in two shots and I thought I was the Ken Griffey Jr. of bird hunting. I wasn't dumb enough to think the streak could last, though.

SANDHILL CRANES HAVE GOT TO BE THE MOST convincing reminder that birds aren't far from dinosaurs. It's hard not to think about that when a fleet of these creatures lumber down from the heavens to land in a barley field, or when their throaty cockles ring out across an expanse of Earth that seems to have no beginning and no end. You might as well be in the Triassic. It follows that these stilted creatures remind me that grouse are ancient, too. It's not like they're once-removed from *Utahraptor* or anything, but there's something prehistoric in the way our beloved gamebirds cock their heads or chuckle nervously from a tree; certainly in the way they explode into flight and set our hearts to thumping. Maybe that's why we crave them so much: no matter how much we think we know them or how close we get, they'll always be separated from us by a few million years. Maybe fishing's the same way.

I was watching these sandhill cranes glide overhead in a steadily increasing downpour and thinking about things I wouldn't normally think of. Like how, for example, it's easy to write off a lack of success when you're new to something. I'd been walking field edges since first light, hoping for sharptails, but all I'd managed to achieve in five hours was a pair of hiking boots that splatted with each step and a pair of pants that were soaked clear up to my belt. I'd found no birds probably because I don't know *how* to find them yet. Novice translates to nothing. But then you've also gotta think that, sometimes, the birds just aren't there. You could have hunted thirty years and known grouse like you know your own bladder and still get duped.

Pretty soon I called an audible and headed for the woods instead, where I busted a covey of young male spruce grouse and filled the vest with two of them. Luck, pure and simple.

Rain crawled up the windshield on the drive back. My new gun was in the backseat, bound to be cleaned and wiped down and doted upon like a favorite child when I got home, tucked into a case far more expensive than I thought cases could be. Just as our fascination and hunger for birds may be among that which is unexplainable—at least in a big, profound sense—so too may our love of fine guns. I'm not calling my first side-by-side a fine gun by any means; it's a simple boxlock with chemically hardened steel and one that a true double enthusiast might scowl at. But you'd probably take a small fortune to buy it off me now.

It's also funny how some people say "Congratulations," when you get a new gun. It's not like I've ushered my progeny into the world or received a promotion at work; in fact I haven't done anything besides make what some could consider a reckless purchase. But maybe that debatably reckless purchase heralds a new level of commitment; I've invested in a tool that will outlive me and may fall into the hands of a child, a grandchild someday. Maybe it'll become part of a collection that my one-day son or daughter will think is infinite, and though they may not know every story of how each one got there, or how it got that nick in the stock, they'll come to find out as I, slowly, with the unspooling years, pass them into their quivering hands. Just like Dad did.

I thought about Dad as I tromped those wetted barley fields, and about how when he handed me those guns he actually handed me something else. Something to chew on during long walks, on cold mornings in the grouse woods; something heavy to tuck inside the game vest and feel bump against you every now and then. Because with each gun comes a modicum of something that is to be respected. An aching call to use it. The duty to use it *well*. I may not hit the next grouse that flushes within range, but at least when I miss I'll do it with a pretty gun.

THE SHAPE OF HARES

I LIKE THE IDEA OF CATCHING SMOKE, and I guess that's why I hunt snowshoe hare.

For one thing, there are few animals as ubiquitously revered by folklore. Over the last several thousand years, from Scottish tomes to Indian fables, hares have popped up in the ink as shapeshifters, tricksters, ushers of change, and portenders, among a good many other things. I won't go so far as to say that hunting them borders on the paranormal, but there is an element of magic to the animal that even the most cantankerous can't deny. I recall a rancher in Wyoming whose world was as black-and-white as an old film print, and for whom the only possible supernatural presence was either the Lord Almighty or the electrical transformer across the highway. He never explained to me why he kept a hare's foot on the dashboard, though.

For another and far more practical thing, hare hunting can be as delightfully challenging as sight-casting to fickle trout or creeping within range of a whitetail buck. If you hunt with a rimfire rifle as I do, the art of the hunt isn't so much in the shooting as it is in seeing the hare before they *realize* that you see them—a tall order even for the eagle-eyed. What you're looking for is a prey species that knows he's the toast of the town for every predator within a hundred miles, and one that won't give up much evidence of their presence besides their outsized tracks in the snow. Even these can be deceiving, though, or at least do uncanny things like disappear in the middle of the forest as though the hare launched himself to space.

My hare hunts generally go one of two ways: either I've got one or two in the vest and feel like I'm getting the hang of it, or I'm bumbling around with a gun that's been loaded since I left the truck and starting to wonder if hares even exist at all. They seem to achieve this dichotomy at will; if there's a day the hares don't want to be found, by God you won't see hide nor hair.

You can't look for the shape of a hare or you'll never see them. The rippled white-and-gray of their coat is nearly indistinguishable from Alaskan snow, and you can walk right past dozens of them in ignorant Elmer Fudd bliss and not even guess it. Your best bet is to look for the tips of their ears, or better yet their tiny eyes which are the approximate size and luster of a musket ball. And, by the way, you're looking for these things in a dark and stoic forest decorated with all of a thousand things that could be a hare. Deadfalls. Spruce cones. Shadows of alder branches. The boreal protects its own.

My hare hunting takes place in a variety of habitats. Usually I like old-growth forest with a steadfast population of white and black spruce, maybe some birch and poplar thrown in, along with a healthy understory of alders and willows. It only takes a few key pieces of hare life history to start to guess where to find them. First, unlike their rabbit cousins, hares do not seek the shelter of dens. Even if it gets atrociously cold. They'll be out at forty degrees below zero, though they'll usually cozy up underneath a spruce tree and be about as active as a cinderblock. For this they need reliable cover. Additionally, hares are mostly nocturnal. They strip bark from willows and nip away any tree buds they can find while the sky is dark (which, of course, is most of the time from October through March in the Last Frontier). I would say that I hunt with this feeding ecology in mind; that I leave the truck at sunrise with a strategy formulated based on where the hares have been feeding and where I, consequently, have a good chance of intercepting them. But the honest answer is that I just start walking zig-zags and hope for the best.

My first hare was as thrilling at twenty-four years old as it would've been if I was eight. It was an overcast day in November. Up to that point, I'd jumped maybe half a dozen hares in as many outings and had pretty much written the things off as impossible, or at least illusory. I'd caught brief snatches of their image—fur as white as the garments worn by angels, eyes sparkling mischievously like marbles—but the actual smoke had slipped cleanly through my fingers. There's a popular Cornish legend suggesting that when a man betrays a pure maiden, she turns into a white hare and follows him for the rest of his days in merciless torment. Nobody but the perpetrator can see this white spectral shape. By that point in my life I was happily married and as far as I knew Emmie was happy, but it does make you wonder. Was the snowshoe hare visible only to me? Was I chasing mirage-water through the forest, spiraling into a torment prescribed for a sin I'd long since forgotten? That's the kind of thing I mean when I say the hunting borders on the paranormal.

In a more practical woodsman sense, though, they are only *wabbits*; a prey species doing their darndest to survive. They've achieved this so effectively that humans write them off as semi-mythical.

I've come to hunt hares exclusively with an open-sighted .22. It started out that way because it was the only gun I had, and it's remained that way because I like the featherlight heft of small shooters and the stillness of creeping through taiga, stalking instead of chasing, allowing the hare his refuges of invisibility and speed. My little Rossi Model 62 is barely larger than a BB gun, but every time

I pull the trigger I feel like I'm standing in the Wyoming driveway, all of eight years old, as Dad hands it to me. I stand by the claim that hare hunting can be as challenging an outdoor pursuit as any, but on top of that it still elicits a childlike surrender that few other things can match. That's one of the things I love most about it; such children's games have the most honest players. Maybe a boy hunting rabbits is all I ever want to be.

Most of the hares I encounter nearly surprise me out of my boots. I often hear them well before I see them, each thump of those oversized feet as sweet as a timpano and as lively as my own pulse. Generally they stop long enough for me to mount the gun, believing with perfect conviction in their perfect camouflage. This is when the cold weather inserts itself to make the whole shooting bit slightly unpredictable; sometimes the firing pin does what it's supposed to do, other times it doesn't and all you get is the scolding plink of a dry fire. If the hare isn't so accommodating, however, you really don't even have time to *think* of mounting the gun (let alone worry about whether it'll fire or not) before they vanish. Or, in the most humiliating of cases, they offer up an easy shot that you just whiff, either because your heart is chugging like a thump keg or because you neglect to accommodate for your rimfire's tendency to shoot about three inches high in close quarters. In a scenario like this, when you've trudged around in the cold for hours and miles on end and just had your pride destroyed, you realize that nothing is so heartbreaking as desire when it leaps away on feet as quiet as a hare's.

These feet really are a marvel of nature. Early Native Americans based the first snowshoes off of them, achieving something that works well enough for us but is really nothing compared to the real thing. The fur on and between a hare's toes is semi-waterproof, and it does such a good job of insulating and 'floating' the hare above the snow that they seem to be gliding. That same fur is also some of the best dry fly material known to man. I use as much of it as possible in my grayling flies, from Fran Betters' classic Usual pattern to the Klinkhåmer Special by Norwegian Hans van Klinken.

Not long ago, I was hunting a new spot off of one of Alaska's loneliest roads. The day began on the same morning this book began, actually; in the dark, in the truck, waiting for sunrise. The sunrise, it turned out, was spectacular, and the ensuing day was the rich blue of a feed store calendar. I zigzagged my way through habitat just riddled with hare tracks, but among the other strange things they do, these footprints will often make you think that the lagomorph-equivalent of the March on Washington's just happened when it was really just two or three animals mucking around. I'd been hunting long and hard enough that my mind had fallen back on a kind of Neanderthalic autopilot, while the yearning for some kind of action had steadily built to a droning sound. It was just as the sun was looping down the opposite hemisphere that I saw one; a big old hare who flitted in between some yearling spruces and gave me a split-second's worth of recognition. Then he was gone.

A story from India speaks of a hare tricking a lion into hunting and eating his own reflection in a well, thus drowning himself. As your hamstrings thrum with pain and your stomach feels as empty as a flat tire, you can't help but wonder if *you're* the one chasing your own reflection now. The passage of your own blood. Then as you work back through, your eyes catch upon a shape just down the hill, and after the fact you can't explain why they looked that way instead of five feet to the left, for example, where they would've seen nothing. It's as if they were puppeted. You raise the gun to your shoulder. It's a long shot, but a shot worth taking. Winter is broken by the neat crack of the rifle, and moments later you heft the plump little leveret and admire his kingly hide just as the Alaskan horizon ignites into magma.

An outing just a few weekends after that was essentially the opposite. By noon, the weight of three hares in my vest was so great that I decided to stop and clean a few of them. Three is my self-imposed limit, so I was heading back to the truck anyway but still had a mile or so to go. I also decided this would be a good chance to practice my fire-making, a skill I hadn't utilized in a while but one that, if you spend a lot of time in the woods, you'd better have sharpened. A match and a section of the newspaper funnies is all it took. You could consider my woodsman ego stroked.

There's yet another story of a hare, this time in Native American lore, that tells of the creature stealing fire. In this yarn, the earth started off cold and dark (which isn't so hard to imagine as I peel my way through the first hare in what feels like ten degrees below zero). Eventually, the Thunderbirds—legendary and divine figures—sent lightning to an island where only weasels lived. As the weasels reveled in their fortune, the people of the world scratched their heads and wondered how they could obtain fire, too. And who do you reckon had the solution? Yep, the hare. He rubbed pine tar into the fur of his head to make it stand up, swam across to the island, and proceeded to participate in a fireside dance by impressing the pants off of the weasels. He danced his way closer and closer to the blaze before sticking his head in the fire, setting the tar alight, and making a mad dash back to the mainland to distribute his booty for the eternal benefit of all. Dastardly, alright.

I got the first hare cleaned and quartered, but by then I couldn't feel my fingers and decided I'd just do the other two at home. And anyway, I've found snowshoe hare to be the best when you let the carcass rest for a few hours. Cleaning and cooling too soon can make the meat about as tough as shoe leather. If you handle and prepare them correctly, though, I know of no other meal quite as satisfying as snowshoe hare. I like them braised low and slow; slow enough that you can enjoy a good glass of Scotch—something smoky like an Ardbeg or a Lagavulin—while the stovetop does its job.

And speaking of drinks, I make a point to carry coffee with me whenever I hunt hares. I keep it in a Stanley thermos and stuff this in the back of my game vest before I set out into the snow. This habit began in the predictable interest of staying warm, or at least pretending, but it's remained intact because it forces me to stop and let my pulse settle down every now and then. The best hare hunters are stationary as much as they are mobile, but I have a hard time keeping still unless I force myself to. Coffee breaks are my answer. They encourage me to see more: more chickadees flitting through the trees, more beauty in the fractal quality of snowflakes, and, most notably, more hares.

Sometimes things go your way. You see the shape of these hares, your rimfire snaps true, and you're teleported immediately to the empire of an eight-year-old. Other times they don't. The flighty hare makes use of all that he's evolved and lives to flee another day.

I've found the best thing to do in a situation like this is to stop, sip some more coffee, and take stock of a few things. Here I am in a version of God's country that I wouldn't bother to appreciate otherwise, and I'm hunting the undisputed master of this land who torments grown men, who outwits the lion, and who steals fire in their spare time. I guess I can't be too disappointed when they make a fool out of me.

PLUTO & PTARMIGAN

I'M STARTING TO WONDER IF PTARMIGAN can live on Pluto. It's hard to say. They live in the rocky wastes of Alaska's Chugach Mountains, where snowfall can surpass nine hundred inches a year and the windchill shoves the mercury to eighty degrees below zero, so really what's the difference? Let's say Pluto had a little more oxygen. Let's say it had liquid water somewhere below its shell of frozen nitrogen. And let's say, just for kicks, that someone important messed with the celestial rheostat to give it some consistent atmospheric pressure. Still, NASA says nothing can live there. I say NASA knows nothing about ptarmigan.

Shadows are drawn long on a March morning. The sun an acetylene torch. There I am looking for ptarmigan, my feet bound to snowshoes, a twenty-gauge double slung over one shoulder, each of my gloved fingers cradling a set of binoculars and the purified world within them. There's a strong wind howling off the rocky spines to the east, thundering down toward the Pacific. Takes most of my heat with it. I stand and gape the way humans do at mountains, at these geological beasts that strip us right down to envy. I'm just a pair of lungs now, trying to comprehend the dizzying space between me and that peak. A mile? Ten? Looking up, aching to be on it.

Similarly distant is the year 1930. On a knoll northeast of Flagstaff, Arizona, on the night of February 18th, Clyde Tombaugh was looking up, too. Tombaugh, a bespectacled twenty-three-year-old with Kansas farm roots and a penchant for homemade telescope building, had been watching and scrupulously photographing the night sky for nearly a year. He wasn't looking for ptarmigan as I was ninety-three years on; he was looking for the ninth planet. Percival Lowell, founder of the Lowell Observatory where Tombaugh would come to be employed, had suggested such a possibility as early as 1902. He'd noticed faint jiggles in the orbits of Neptune and Uranus and believed these to be caused by a colossal, trans-Neptunian planet. His life's mission, which lurched to a halt in 1916 with a fatal stroke, was to confirm this hunch.

Speaking of hunches, I'm following one of my own: ptarmigan like the wind. Short of an early spring, wind is the only thing that can expose their favorite foods of dwarf birch, willow, and overwintered berries. Here it's available in gale-force quantities, and I spend the better part of a morning picking my way across exposed rock slopes and glassing the tight quarters of alder thickets.

Nada.

That's what Clyde Tombaugh said, too, for countless nights leading up to that February of 1930. In all that time, he'd been religiously documenting the outer fringes of our solar system with a thirteen-inch astrograph and an aptly named blink comparator. Take a few photos of the night sky, compare them to see if you can spot any anomalies. You could imagine Tombaugh playing a hardcore version of 'Spot the Difference' and not be far off; he'd flick back and forth between images using the comparator with such tenacity that it had to become mind-numbing after a while. By the time Tombaugh left the observatory and started teaching navigation to the Navy in 1943, it's estimated that he looked at over ninety-million star images. None would prove so interesting, however, as the two he compared on February 18th—the first taken on January 23rd, 1930; the second from a week later. The pinhole-sized, traveling blip they revealed turned out to be Percival Lowell's guessed-at-but-never-confirmed planet, slowly crawling its way across a 248-year orbit around the Sun. The traveling blip turned out to be Pluto.

It's only after the fact that I can compare looking for ptarmigan to looking for Pluto. Staring down thousands of acres that *could* hold birds. Billions and billions of stars, said Carl Sagan. After a while it all looks the same. Rocks. Snowdrifts. Alder branches scrawled into avian shapes. Spot the difference. I keep marching onward, reciting the litany that *boots kill birds, boots kill birds*. Finally there they are, two miles in. Stars with plumage brighter than snow. Eyes like tungsten. Difference spotted.

My gun gets up as the covey does, dropping one then another. Before the reek of cordite clears I'm upon them, rolling their warm heft in gloved hands, cleaning blood from angelic feathers. I hate killing them. Hate killing anything. My kind says we're doing it out of some primal instinct to eat meat and to be predatory; to kill is to appreciate and to save in some roundabout way. That's all true, but then a lot of things are true. Doesn't make them easier.

My mind dashes irregular orbits like that when I hunt. Snowshoes crackling, head a mile up. I return to the truck with more than I started with; questions, calories burnt, heft in the game vest. Three ptarmigan. All willows from the same covey.

The Scots called these birds *tármachan* for the croaking sound that they make, mostly during breeding season. The name held out until the 1600s, when the Greek *ptéron* (meaning 'feather') was sewn in. They come from the genus *Lagopus*, nestled within a New World clade of grouse species which includes the sharp-tailed grouse, the blue grouse, and the ruffed grouse. It's not clear exactly how the ptarmigans diverged from their lowland brethren, but a fossil record of bones and ancient gizzard stones suggests it began during the Pleistocene; an epoch that emerged two-and-a-half million years ago and was characterized by global glaciation, low sea levels, and lush microregions. Birds in the vast, green swathes of Beringia (about a hundred miles north of where I'm standing) expanded into new niches, many of them high above treeline, and over the slow crawl of time they developed a good many adaptations for dealing with the harsh environment they found there.

I'm looking at most of these traits on the tailgate, in fact, as I break for lunch: a chameleon-esque skin of snow-white feathers (rusty brown-red in the summertime); heavily insulated feet; short, stout bills; blood-red eye combs like those of a chicken. They're faint right now, but give it a month and those combs'll burst like crowns. The males will dance and croak. The hens will lay eggs.

I could go on thinking about all of the prehistory contained within the ptarmigan's wings. I could contemplate the *Archaeopteryx* and *Confuciusornis* species that, at one time long, long ago, bridged the gap between dinosaur and bird and gave rise to the grouse which gave rise to the ptarmigan. An iterative cycle; a process of change and upheaval and rebirth like rocks melting and cooling and amassing into planets. Some things move quickly. Life and geology do not. I could wonder about all of it. Or I could go hunting some more.

I take a quick nap in the driver's seat and tootle higher up into the pass. Out there off the highway it looks like Pluto. No one's ever been to the icy planet—no human object has been closer than 7,750 miles, actually—but here the rocks and the snow cleaved raw by the wind suggest a harshness beyond this world. Pluto's average surface temperature is four hundred degrees below zero. It takes five and a half hours for the light of the sun to reach it. Scientists say there may be an ocean of liquid water somewhere in its inner core, but as of now it's guarded by cryovolcanoes and spires of methane ice as tall as the Empire State Building. Wild.

Until Pluto was discovered, it was thought to be huge. Big enough to influence the orbit of other planets, anyway. Subsequent investigation proved only to shrink it; by 2006, astronomers decided it was more like an object in the Kuiper Belt—a doughnut of frozen space debris on the outer perimeter of our solar system—than any other planet. Hence, its status was changed to "dwarf-planet" by the International Astronomical Union in August of that year to the lasting chagrin of many of the world's astronomers (a good proportion of whom were peevishly excluded from the decision in the first place).

Dwarf-planet or not, of course I'm not actually suggesting that ptarmigan can live on Pluto. Nothing can. I'm not educated enough to tell you what would happen to *me* if I tried trekking across its methane-and-nitrogen surface with snowshoes and a shotgun, but suffice it to say that my death would be quick and painless and I'd probably resemble a Mountain House meal. Here on Earth, in the mountains, the wind batters my eardrums. Snowflakes become weaponized. In some spots my snowshoes cut the ice and give me purchase, in others I'm a human kite, my game vest rippling in full canvas. At one point a helicopter whines overhead. Probably hauling skiers or snowboarders from the lodge down the valley. Every finger up there pointed down at me, the little orange blip, wondering which screw came loose.

A mile in, I turn around, now facing the wind and battling it foot for foot. The errand feels both futile and dangerous now. Wind ripping my heat. Layers useless. Any farther and I might not come back. Just ptarmigan hunting but it feels like interstellar travel now.

Other people hunt the mountain passes closer to town. Five hours west where trailheads actually exist and are marked either by signs or by other vehicles. Skiers and snowboarders and bird hunters that show up as fluorescent strings of pearls up and down the slopes. You know there are birds there but then so does everyone else. Here it's not so easy. Here there are no trailheads, no directions, no confirmations. If anyone's hunted it seriously they've been smart enough to keep their mouth shut about it.

I think about that and a sense of camaraderie overcomes me. Someone else. Maybe many. Before and after. Hiking on boots or snowshoes, clinging to a shotgun and the theories of ptarmigan habitat preference, same as me. Someone plying the dark and the unknown and letting go of the handrail and trudging into the wind, seeing where it all goes. Looking for Pluto, looking for ptarmigan. Doesn't matter which because maybe both are improbable, yet both exist.

It's about then that the birds get up, four or five of them. Rock ptarmigan. Wings catching the gale like thrust, rudders blinking. There all along in the land of the lifeless, a place where it's hard to say if it's heaven or hell or ptarmigan country, at least until you find what you're looking for. Difference spotted again. Now the birds cackle like thieves and it takes me a moment to come to, but when I do I send a Hail Mary not to the dark void of space but to the white comet of a single bird. The inner calculus to catch its path bursts from the saurian cockpit of my brain. I'm a Tombaugh-at-the-telescope. Velocity, rate of change.

Going . . .

Match it.

Vanishing into the cosmos of the mountains . . .

Blot the shape.

MINK

THE BOY SWALLOWS MORNING INTO HIS LUNGS. It's half a mile to the bridge from the house, another quarter down the creek where his traps are laid. All through the dark. He takes it singing softly to himself, the flashlight in his hand cutting the night open and zipping it closed behind him. He likes that the air tastes unused.

The first mink he caught was an accident. He'd never told anyone, but it was. The day before school started back up after Christmas he'd dug a big hole in the side of the creek and set some carrots back there and guarded the entrance with a Conibear. Hoping for a muskrat. He checked the trap every day after school and basketball practice and each day it'd come up empty until one day it didn't. That night his father had driven him home in the van and stopped along the dirt road by the bridge and the boy hopped out, basketball sneakers white and phosphorescent, bare shins parting the cattails and only the broken bores of headlights to show the way. In the dark he felt for the trap, careful and tactile as a raccoon as his hands found clay, found the creek.

Finally he grasped fur, a wet bundle of it laddered by ribs, and he grabbed the thing and hoisted it and the moment the musk entered his nostrils he knew it was mink. Never smelled it before but he knew.

He pulled against the trap wire but the stake was anchored and wouldn't budge, so he got up and leapt back toward the van. Fell into the marsh. What he must've looked like to Dad back there. Sneakers now black filling with cold. He wanted to shout but didn't and he turned and grabbed the trap, grabbed the mink, and pulled until his little spine groaned and the rebar came up. He dragged it back and he crossed the barbed wire fence and threw open the van door.

"I caught a mink."

Dad looks back, half-grinning.

"Had a feeling."

Maybe he knew it was an accident, but he didn't say anything.

This one won't be an accident, the boy thinks, almost a year on, wading through the dark now. The day before, he'd gone down and set the trap and it was destined for mink this time, everything about it from the tangle stake to the mink musk and the crawdad oil smeared inside the hole, the trap a one-and-a-half coilspring dyed black as wine.

The creek was spring-fed and it wended north to south through cattle pastures and corn fields before it finally dumped into the river. At one time it held trout but no longer. Nowadays just chubs and carp. And the perch he caught one time. Russian olives gorge themselves like old men on the banks, their branches clasping witchlike at the sky and turning the creek bottoms ashy like it was always dusk. Beneath those trees coons and mink and foxes wander and whitetail deer pass without shadows.

The boy and his brother have explored most of it. It ran through the back of the family farm and where that ends in barbed wire, they just hop the fence and keep going. Eventually they ask permission to trap it from the farmers next door. Some places are familiar and well-worn; the pool above the bridge, for example, or the muskrat pond where Hank went through the ice, or the spot where Dad wanted to build a duck blind. Others are far-flung; eerie and hostile yet deliciously uncharted. Tales of beaver and bobcats in those darkened willows to the south. *Here be dragons*.

It was too early in the year to be setting traps. Middle of October, a full month before furs really primed up, but they got a screaming blizzard a couple of days ago and the boy tells himself that'll be enough to do it. Never mind that fur thickens based on deteriorating daylight rather than weather. He sets the trap anyway and doesn't stop to think maybe he's doing it because he's not planning on catching anything. Maybe he's doing it because flukes can take a long time to happen twice.

That next morning there he is stepping into the creek, boots sloshing, fingers feeling that sting of cold, his jaw set. The wendigos of the night watch him beyond the reach of the flashlight beam.

His heart snaps up into his throat when he sees the trap is gone. Just vacant clay-bank the color of bone now. He sets the flashlight in the grass where it throws grotesqueries and he reaches out with his trowel and finds the stake anchored in deep water. Tap of steel on steel. The boy's skin prickling with gooseflesh now Then he finds the tangle stake and manages to hook the wire and it all comes up like the relic of a sunken ship. Chain, trap—*Mink*.

A little female slickened and oily-black, the white bib of her chin smeared with clay. Faint sour reek of glands, a smell only the grave can forget. Now he's drinking the air, trying to swallow it, don't pour it out, because mink don't happen every day and he knows he'll grow old but right now he's young and awake while the world is sleeping.

CHASING THE DARK

These steelhead—*Aashát,* in the indigenous Tlingit tongue—have hatched from globules no bigger than a pea, survived perils ranging from mergansers to salmon sharks, and traveled hundreds if not thousands of miles under their own propulsion to be here. All I had to do was board a flight to southeast Alaska in early May.

Several months before, on the opposite side of a long winter, I'd managed to drum up some interest in a few magazine articles about the steelhead in this place. This is how it goes: you send inquiries to magazines first to make sure you can get the thing published, then you send Hail Marys to lodges hoping for a sponsorship of some kind. To write is to live within constant rejection, so you never actually believe any of it will land. It's just fun to imagine. When it *does* land, though, and people actually say yes to your harebrained ideas, you feel like you've just successfully roped a train. The next step is to figure out the logistics of the trip and make good on all those promises you made.

The glaring problem with my original proposition was that I

couldn't do a southeast Alaska steelhead trip alone. In addition to competent writing, magazines these days appreciate fancy photography—the level of which I could not hope to attain by doing things solo with a self-timer. Emmie is a professional photographer, but I knew she'd scalp me if I put her through a week of steelhead fishing. That and I can't afford her going rate anymore.

This left one person: Ryan Kelly, the Rainbow King. The next obstacle was that he was in Missouri.

I was driving out for a weekend of trout fishing when I called him. He picked up on the first or second ring, which was surprising because most of the time he doesn't pick up at all. He's got a three-year-old son and a demanding job in the military. I'm not sure which is more troublesome.

Anyway, I pitched him my idea and figured, not unlike with the magazine editors and lodge owners I'd sent pleas to months earlier, that he'd pretend to think about it for a few days and finally let me off easy by saying he just couldn't make it work. I would've understood. I'd preemptively understood. I was a little floored, then, when he said he'd *seriously* think about it, then a few days later when he said he'd ask the wife about it, and then a few more days later when he said he was in. Just like that.

I booked plane tickets during my lunch break at school the next week. By the following Monday, I'd brought in my fly-tying kit, and by Tuesday, students were finding pink dubbing, grouse feather tips, zebra-striped rubber legs, and even size-10 Czech nymph hooks within the pages of their shoddily graded research papers. Occasionally students would gather around my desk at lunchtime or after school, marveling at the grown man who was happily ignoring his assigned duties and the phone ringing on the windowsill in favor of the miniscule hook pinched before him.

One of them probably asked me why it took me so long to tie those stupid little stonefly things, and why I was makin' 'em pink.

The Anchorage airport in May is full of fly rods. It's not every person that's got one, but it's pretty close. Some of them strut like horses because they're going on a fishing trip; others wander dejectedly, faces grim like they've just been diagnosed with stomach cancer, because they just got *back*. We all pass one another, at once anonymous yet joined in solemn brotherhood. We are the enlightened; the caste that knows steelhead exist, that this is their season. Occasionally we'll nod at one another, acknowledging, but mostly it's just a fleeting confluence of gazes and no-grins pleated over skulls that frenzy for the anadromous.

Snatches of conversation in the terminal go like this:

"Lost a thirty-eight incher in a logjam."

"We tried soft eggs this year, don't know if they helped."

"River was skinny as a meth-head while we were there. They're gonna be gettin' rain this week, though. Anybody headed there now ought to be in for a treat."

Steelhead, at least when you're headed toward them, have the pleasing effect of most depressants. By that I mean you can board a plane and sit back and relax, and you really don't care what happens around you so long as you get to a sea-run rainbow trout at the end of it.

Turbulence like a bad circus ride? Sure. Two-year-old kid screaming like he just got his fingernails yanked out? No problem. I'll take the obese seatmate that smells like a cleaved onion too, thanks.

I met Ryan in Juneau. Since there are only a couple of jets in and out of our destination per day, his flight from Seattle had to wait for the passengers of mine to flurry onboard before taking off. We snagged seats next to one another and chatted the way old friends do. It was the same old Ryan sitting there next to me; same reticence, same gladiator gleam in his eye that I'd seen those years ago when we chased cohos, trout, grayling together—the gleam that suggested he wanted nothing more than to fish himself to death. The world changes and so does your life but fishing buddies rarely do. We landed in a growing drizzle, the grandeur of mountains and ocean dulled by thick sheets of cloud.

Gravel popped in the undercarriage of a rental car as we headed into the village. The upholstery smelled like a rainforest. We grabbed a few sundries at the grocery store, checked into our lodge, and headed back toward the river with a few hours of daylight to spare. The four or so vehicles we passed in all that time waved like they knew us and hadn't seen us since high school. This is why I love small towns. They're like good dogs, most of them. Unassuming. Passionately friendly.

The moment we arrived at the river was a big one for me. This is a legendary fishery and I'd been planning this escapade for a year. Now here we were. The rest of the world fell away; all I could feel was the throbbing potential for steelhead.

We fished for a couple hours and got a feel for the river, which, as those voices had suggested in the Anchorage airport, was rising steadily with the pounding rain. We weren't alone out there. Nearly every pool was bestatued by a fisherman, some by two or three. We passed them all, nodding, muttering, seeking our own water. Eventually we found it and I managed to land a bright hen steelhead on an egg-sucking leech. She was maybe eight pounds and pretty as could be; the kind of fish that makes you sit back a little and think about what you're doing, and maybe why.

I think one of the things about anadromous fish that so fascinates us is that they lead such big lives. Take a second to imagine it: a puny little steelhead fry wiggling around somewhere out there, no bigger than your little finger. In just a year or two they'll swim out into the open ocean the same way a college kid finally says goodbye to Mom and Dad. They'll head off into the world and if they return it means they've made it and that they've achieved everything and exactly what they were meant to. This is something humans rarely do, so, naturally, we envy the hell out of it.

ALL FISH ARE, TO SOME EXTENT, sensitive to light. Steelhead especially. The very best time to catch one is right at or in close proximity to sunrise and sunset; just about when darkness either cedes authority or takes up the reins. You can catch them in the middle of the day, sure, but your chances are higher at low light. They feel safer, the water's slightly cooler, and, ideally, they've forgotten most of the angler harassment they endured the day before. With sunrise being at something like five in the morning for that region of Alaska, Ryan and I knew we'd be in for some early wakeup calls. You want to chase the dark off the water, so to speak, so we planned to rise at three, get prepped, hike in, and be fishing through headlamps about as soon as civil twilight began.

The lodge was quiet and dark that next morning. The smell of mildew hung in the air from half a dozen pairs of waders smoldering in the mud room.

Another angler was already up, checking his stock portfolio. We'd met him the night before and, though I don't remember his name now, he was part of a gaggle of friends from Pennsylvania and Florida who'd been doing this trip every year for the last eight. This river invites that kind of devotion; later in the week I met a Frenchman who'd been returning since the early '90s.

To tell you the truth, if I'd have been by myself I probably wouldn't have gone out that morning. It was still dumping rain, and a quick check of the Geological Survey's stream gauge revealed that the river was approaching dangerous levels. It was iffy if we were going to be able to cross, and to me that represented the perfect excuse to sleep in, call it an easy morning, and interview some people for my articles. Luckily Ryan saved me from wimping out. He's good at that.

That first day was full of rain. Cold—startlingly cold—and clammy and relentless. Our souls huddled together in it, first as we strung up our rods and then as we hiked upstream, reminding ourselves that this was steelhead weather, and steelhead weather brings steelhead. Boots squelching through mud, the trail more of a suggestion. Waist deep in the stream. Logs smooth like mammoth tusks.

Morning passed. Ryan almost hooked a fish but didn't. I got some interesting photos of the rainforest. Moss on trees. Steller's jays.

Steelhead weather brings steelhead—steelhead weather brings steelhead—

Lunchtime. We struggled upriver, wallowing in snow that was up to our belly buttons, climbing like toddlers under downed trees. We knew the trail ended about two miles up from the bridge, and though this distance was academic on the map, it felt like forever out there. Finally we reached a pool that became our favorite; a starting point, a lunching spot, an ace-in-the-hole, a coffee break. Ryan managed to land his first steelhead there toward mid-afternoon, and though I almost bungled the net job, I didn't. I guess it was a fish he was meant to have.

Someone's first steelhead is a big deal. It ain't like catching your first bluegill. Steelhead are said to be the fish of a thousand casts, and maybe that number is dampened a little in this place, but it's still respectable. Even if they're the fish of five hundred casts, to catch one means that you've *made* those five hundred casts, and that you've made them in such a way as to be effective, and that you've braved the elements that steelhead find conducive to procreation and that you've outwitted a fish notorious for being supernaturally moody. A special occasion to be sure, and one to remember for a long time, probably forever.

We caught a few other nice steelhead that day before heading in at dusk. The fish weren't all that big, but when you're talking wild steelhead, you don't complain. Back at the lodge we were filled with aches and the kind of bone-deep cold that only hot showers could take care of. We hung our waders and soggy rain jackets and knew we'd be sliding into them damp the next morning.

The lodge had a big living room with fish mounts and a view of the ocean. I sat there staring at the ceiling for a while. You could say I was reliving the day, but more than anything I was trying to make sense of the fact that it happened at all. It was my first 'destination' article assignment, a taste of the big leagues in my mind, and here we'd tinkered a trip together that hadn't flaked, hadn't flopped, and hadn't been cancelled due to some miscellaneous act of God. It defied expectation.

About then, the party from Pennsylvania and Florida showed up, shaking off the rain.

"That water is *hiiggghhh*." The stock trader whistled impressively. "How'd you guys do?"

I was about to say something cryptic, maybe misleading, when Ryan jumped in.

"It was awesome. I got my first steelhead."

Right on, man, I thought. Right on. No sense holding it close to the chest. You've got the badge now. Let 'er fly.

Pretty soon we were tying more flies—black woolly buggers because we thought we'd figured out a pattern—and you could just see the old fire, reawakened, in Ryan's eye. First steelhead. No goin' back. By the time we called it quits it was pushing eleven o'clock. Alarms would sound four hours later.

I had to envy Ryan's passion. He was here to fish, and by God he was going to wring out every second of it that he could. Like all those stream miles we'd shared when he lived in Alaska. I laid there listening to his snoring, wondering if I had what it took to keep up with him; if I could do this for another five days, sun-up to sun-down; if I even cared enough.

Just before sleep bagged me, though, I realized I didn't have much of a choice.

ONE MINUTE I'M A KID PLUNKING EARTHWORMS and the next I'm twenty-six and contemplating steelhead; one moment our heads are hitting the pillow that second night, and next thing we know the week's unravelling beneath us.

We fought the river as it rose each day. Rain hammered us for the first couple, but it would relent occasionally and the clouds would part like curtains to reveal the sun and blue skies. We'd bask in these ephemeral heavens. We had fly rods in our hands, everything we could ever need on our backs, and more often than not we'd be staring down a jag of steelhead that were so big and numerous they looked like salmon. All of the world's problems could be solved from right there.

Fish to hand didn't come easy—turns out our supposed theory about black woolly buggers was all wrong—but they weren't impossible, either.

We'd hang around our favored pool for most of the mornings, waiting for fresh charges of steelhead to move in, fishing our way downstream and then hiking back up. One day we fished down and back about five times. Usually we'd have a coffee break and we'd always take lunch.

Eventually—around day three or four, I think—the weather came to be dominated by partial sun rather than those wool-sock clouds that leaked rain. It was a welcomed change. The river finally starting dropping and I could hear the echoes of all those voices in the Anchorage airport:

"Anyone headed there now will be in for a treat."

They weren't talking about the surge of rain. Well, they *were*, but they were mostly talking about what would happen after it stopped. The river had been low and clear and not very conducive to steelhead movement for weeks leading up to our arrival. Then all of the sudden, the rain came and water levels rose and the stream temps dropped within the range that steelhead like to party in (somewhere between thirty-nine and forty-two degrees Fahrenheit.) Now, with the atmospheric spigot turned off, the river would likely hover in the correct temperature range, while its levels would slowly drop and constrict steelhead to fishable water. In short, it was an ideal set of conditions, and our days somehow got longer and longer just trying to capitalize on our improbable luck.

The rainforest, once stern and bruiting for two guys from plains country, became an acquaintance. Not one you knew a lot about, but one you'd accepted and that you felt had maybe accepted you. At least to the point of tolerance.

The whole place was alive. That became evident the more we sat still. Never mind the steelhead; several times at lunch, a mink would flow through the roots of an upturned tree nearby and we'd stare, not a word between us. Twice we watched a river otter surface like a submarine, its fur slick as oil. Birdsong was constant, the workday chatter of varied thrushes and fox sparrows pinging out through the trees, coming from all directions. Occasionally you'd see the musicians themselves. I came to sit still for longer periods of time just trying to notice these things. I'd look for otter tracks. I'd watch the dippers as they scoured for mayfly nymphs. Ryan, on the other hand, seemed to just fish harder. He'd work through the pools once, twice, three times, and then when we'd hiked a mile downstream he'd reel up his line and say something like, "I'd like to try that hole up top again." So we'd hike.

I'd begrudge him every so often, silently. I couldn't write a very good article, in my view, if we just hammered the river without regard. If I never took any time to reflect. This was a place that needed care; a delicate hand. Piles of articles and travel brochures had already been published about the steelhead here, touting their abundance not for its own sake, but for the number of clients you could fit in a drift boat.

Double-digit fish days.

Fish to forty inches and beyond.

That sort of thing.

I wasn't about to complain about the oodles of steelhead we could cast to in a day, but I wasn't going to play the broken piano, either. The problem is that travelling anglers get so caught up in the hype that they forget these are steelhead at all; that elsewhere they are the cherished fish of maybe *ten* thousand casts rather than a thousand or five hundred or even just ten; that elsewhere, these days, they are imperiled.

Still, I followed Ryan. Call it nostalgia. Call it blind faith. He was the King, after all, and I owed much of my obsession to him.

Steelhead mired our dreams at night, each one playing out to the ratcheting click of things unfurling; our reels, our minds. We'd rise to the wails of alarms, eyes stinging, bones pleading, up into the moldy dark to the kitchen where we'd make the first pot of coffee, where we'd heat the burritos and scarf them down and move like arthritic dogs to load everything in the car. There we were in that slice of time, driving mindlessly to the gabble of radio, following headlamps that cut open the forest, wandering the river like mink. Chasing the dark just as hard as we could.

THE SECOND-TO-LAST DAY IS WHEN THINGS REALLY started to happen. We'd slowly worked out the fly patterns that caught fish, more or less. We also figured out things like where those fish would be holding, how to approach them, how long of a leader to use, and how much lead split-shot to crimp on.

Things began that day, like usual, at our pool. That sounds pretty casual as I write it, but in the moment I remember I was festering like a splinter.

Every muscle ached and I was running on twelve hours of sleep for the last week. Little things irritated me at first and then infuriated me; how I was the only one with a net, how I always had to be the one to heat lunch, how Ryan would somehow crave the exact opposite of what I wanted. One second I'd want to fish a run carefully and off he'd go blasting downstream; the next he'd stop heron-still and cast to the same fish for an hour, maybe two, while I just wanted to see more of the river.

Anyway, curmudgeon Joe was tampered a little after I'd caught a nice steelhead on a Copper John nymph that morning. One that

I'd tied for grayling fishing. Then about ten o'clock Ryan hooked a fish and, in the commotion, an absolute whopper of a steelhead sidled out from under a log to see what was happening. He took on my first cast, and for the first time all week, we were doubled up. Ryan got his netted in short order, but mine was big enough that I couldn't do a whole lot right away. We danced in a stalemate for a while; the fish trying to bulldog back under the log, me walking the tightrope of just enough pressure to keep him out but not enough to snap the tippet. Just when I thought I had him, and I went to scoop the net under him—Ryan was holding his fish in the water on the gravel bar—he took off and the angle was all wrong and the hook popped out. *Kapow.*

Well—that blew a fuse. I had all of a million accusations to throw at the world, at Ryan, but in the end it came right down to my own fault. I'd gotten caught up in the hype; I wanted a steelhead double to snap a photo of for my article. Of course you don't see that when the blood's running thick through your eyes, though.

We fished downstream like we did any other day. I was moving fast just wanting it to be over. I'd put big stretches between Ryan and I; sometimes a couple hundred yards, sometimes farther. Later in the afternoon, Ryan hooked a fish way upstream and when I heard his shout I could've killed him. Just call it a day, for Pete's sake. I had an article to write and I couldn't do it following his lunatic ass up and down the river. And hell—I hooked that behemoth a half hour ago and where was he with the net? I hoofed it upstream for something like a quarter mile before I finally got to him.

It's a horrible thing to say now, but I wished that fish would just snap him off. Give him a taste of that ugly plummeting feeling; make it so I wasn't the only one. But that didn't happen. He got the fish in a spot where I could net it, so I did, and he whooped like he always did, like a kid who just won a baseball trophy.

Same old Ryan.

Finally, near dark, things went my way. I cast a pink stonefly that I tied in my classroom all those months ago to a coin-slot of fast water. A bright hen steelhead obliged the cast and stuff happened like it's supposed to and Ryan netted her. It turned out to be the longest fish we'd seen thus far, and one that threw me from despondency to euphoria.

You lose a fish and you might as well kill yourself, then a half hour later you land one and the world is yours, there in the palm of your hand like a seed. This is what those faces in the airport know, the glowing and the forsaken. Those heading home and those leaving it. They know what it is to chase steelhead and to play with fire. They know how it all tends to shake things loose inside you.

The fish lay panting in the net and we both stared and then Ryan grinned from ear to ear and held out his fist. I knocked it with my own. My knuckles said something along the lines of, "I'm sorry for being a butthead earlier, and I'm actually enjoying the hell out of life right now," so that my mouth didn't have to.

Same old Ryan. Same old King. The world changes but fishing buddies rarely do. Thank God.

We stopped at the bar on the way back to the lodge and had a beer each. Ryan showed me how to play cribbage.

LAST MORNING. BY THAT POINT OUR ROOM SMELLED like a gym locker, and geez do I feel bad for the housekeeper. It was one of the best days of my life.

It began in the dark and got lighter slowly. There wasn't a cloud in the sky and the first couple of pools we fished were occupied by an otter that seemed to be following us. Then the sun burst through the trees, bright as an arc welder, and we found ourselves looking at a group of steelhead, each big like car bumpers.

Ryan gave them a burst of casts before moving on. I moved in and picked out a particular fish—a lithe, brutish shape that looked more like a taimen than anything else—and stood there casting to her like an idiot for twenty minutes. After a while it became mindless. Drop a cast. Watch the fly. Watch the group of steelhead part like the Red Sea to avoid it. I had two or three split-shots tucked under my lip—a "split-shot dip," as Ryan called it—so I added a couple and tried again and again.

It was one of those things that, the longer you do it, the less likely it seems it'll work. But somehow it did. The big ol' steelhead queen wormed over from under the logjam and I dropped a cast and watched her great white maw flash once and, whadda ya know, she had my pink stonefly clamped in her mouth.

Off my heart went, thumping like a phonebook in a dryer. Off *I* went, trying to stay on two feet and not lose the fish. That's really all you become. A violent rip of synapses just trying to keep a tight line. Everything else zapped from your mind.

She filled the net when Ryan scooped it underneath her. There's a lot more to say about her, but telling people about your big old fish is like getting an honor roll sticker for your kid; nobody really cares. Suffice it to say that she taught me a little bit. Actually, she taught me a lot. Like how to be patient. How to live fiercely. How to take the good with the bad and live in the moment because one day we'll all be dead. Maybe I knew that all along, it just took a three-foot steelhead to bring it to light. I let her go and I stopped fishing after that. I was full.

Ryan couldn't understand why I'd want to quit early and leave a whole bunch of water unfished after only one steelhead; I couldn't understand why he just couldn't be satisfied. But on that final day we settled it. It wasn't something we agreed to disagree on, or even discussed at all, it was just one of those things we accepted in our own ways. I'd sit on gravel bars listening to the birds as we moved downstream; he'd fish the pool in front of me with cast after cast.

"These might be the last steelhead I'll ever catch," he'd say in justification, which is probably not true but it does make you think for a second.

If I knew this was my last day to chase the dark shapes of steelhead, would I fish like hell, or would I savor every last bit of it? Would I notice things like otter tracks on the bank or fox sparrows in the trees? I think I would. I think I'd drink it all down.

Aashát. Steelhead. A fish, not a number.

Kóoshdaa. River otters watching it all.

Xáats'. Skies so blue it hurts.

Steelhead aren't steelhead without the rest, and all of it's here. It's not touted or hyped or printed on glossy pamphlets; it's just a river that can smack your jaw wide open if you're smart enough to let it. The trees creak and whisper in the lightest of winds, the varied thrushes ping like sonar high in the canopy, and you imagine just how many millions of acres of this you'll never hear about, where in nameless backwaters those little steelhead hatch and embark. Their lives go on without you, but you know your own could never go on without them.

Ryan got his moment, too. It was after lunch in the bright sun and we were hiking back upstream and spotted a ragged old male noodling around in a deep pool. Ryan crossed, got into position, and I directed his casts from above. The fish took quickly; Ryan played it quickly, too, and we got it into the net. That may not have been the last steelhead of his life, but he'll be hard-pressed to catch one more stunning. You don't realize how much you want a good friend—a best friend—to catch the fish of their life until they do.

We flew home the next day. In Anchorage we got off and wandered the terminal, faces grim and thirsting like those I'd seen so long ago. We were the ones coming back now. Back to work, back to life, back to things governed by time and made of plastic. It felt like we'd been gone a lot longer than a week.

When it was time to leave each other—Ryan for a connecting flight to St. Louis, me for an Uber bound for the apartment across town—our words were few. Most of them were out on the river. Still, I thanked him for making the trip of a lifetime happen, and for making sure the writing that I'd do was honest. I thanked him for never changing.

He grinned and we shook hands and I like to think that he slept on the plane ride home. That he dreamed of steelhead.

THE CALCULUS OF SPEY

Almost two hundred years after the first Spey rods were used, I stood attempting to cast one toward the idea of Alaskan steelhead.

The rod itself is thirteen and a half feet long; perhaps a better tool for a pole vaulter than a fish enthusiast. It's heavy, like rebar, but man will it sling line—even in my unpracticed, untuned hands. I ordered it back in January, and after a convoluted process of supply chain shortages and rising unemployment rates, it finally arrived on the doorstep in March. The weeks in between were filled with hours of Spey casting videos on repeat. I'd stand in front of them, totally transfixed, totally oblivious to anything else (mainly work), and attempt to mimic the motions required for a commendable Snap-T or a Double Spey using a broomstick.

Late April washed over Alaska and we welcomed it like a loved one back from war. On a Monday, my friend Andy inquired about my weekend plans. By Friday we were shuttling south to the Kenai Peninsula, chromed spring steelhead dancing in our minds.

I fish with Andy for a couple of reasons. First and foremost, the guy's just fun to be around. He's selfless but not self-righteous, confident but not arrogant, he talks only when he's got something to say, and he's amassed a variety of neat perspectives on the world which he shares with total and utter conviction. That and he's one hell of a fisherman, not to mention one who's versed in the intricacies of Spey fishing. He knew about my recent purchase and assured me that this wouldn't just be a fishing trip. It would be a few days of casting lessons.

THE HISTORY OF SPEY FISHING IS ALMOST AS interesting as the act itself. The best compendium of this that I can find is Arthur Lingren's exhaustive *The Spey Cast or Welsh Throw: History in Great Britain, Roots in British Columbia, and Popularity in North America*. Lingren is apparently tenacious in pursuit of both angling history and wild anadromous fish. Anyhow, Spey fishing itself was originally known as the 'Welsh throw,' and the best that anyone can tell is that the cast first appeared in print in the Irishman Edward Fitzgibbon's 1850 work, *The Book of Salmon*. Mention it is about all he did; Fitzgibbon gave away little on how to execute the cast and didn't get around to it before he drank himself to death in 1857. He long promised to write about his experiences in intoxication, as well, but he didn't get around to that, either.

Thankfully, sporting editor Francis Francis (his parents struggled with originality) shed more light on the Welsh throw in the latter part of the 19th Century. He also helped introduce brown trout to New Zealand and Tasmania, but that's another story. Francis describes the cast as one born out of necessity; anglers could not cast the typical fly lines with rocks or shrubbery to their backs and thus required a novel method of propulsion. No backcast, no whipping line back and forth. He even provided an illustration. In those early days it took on the nickname of 'Spey casting,' even though it was practiced on many other rivers besides the Spey. It took a few more decades before the cast was described in useful and actionable detail—the credit for this goes to Eric Taverner in his *Salmon Fishing* of 1931.

While single-handed fly casting involves whipping the rod back and forth to generate 'load' (a term for the energy stored within a rod which can then be transmitted into launching a fly), Spey—or, two-handed casting—uses the surface tension of line on the water to achieve this load. You're not standing in the water and waving a stick, as John Gierach would say of single-handers; you're making what is essentially a giant roll cast. Per the cast's origins, this can be done despite bankside obstacles behind you. And, it turns out, with a rod of optimal length—say, between eleven and fourteen feet—you can launch flies a heck of a lot farther than you can on single-handed rods. (There are reports from the late 1800s of anglers making sixty-five-yard Spey casts).

This latter bit of trivia translates well to large river systems; exactly the thoroughfares that anadromous fish such as salmon and steelhead utilize. I would elaborate upon that but, owing to a leaden foot and dry roads, Andy and I reached the river far earlier than expected. No time for history when it's time to saddle up.

Carrying a two-handed rod is a symbol. Like driving a Lamborghini. Laypeople may not know exactly what they're looking at when you first pull up, but they know it's special in some kind of way. Elite. Enlightened. Refined. Fly anglers are kind of that way in general, or at least act like it, but Spey gurus are a whole new echelon. Spey rods don't necessarily symbolize success, but they do represent a higher-than-average level of devotion. A commitment to the swung fly and *only* the swung fly; an imposition of strict limitations.

The first afternoon of casting went about like I expected. Working the rod felt like trying to wrestle a lengthy shaft of PVC pipe, and it took me a while to get the hang of letting the line slink through my fingers in the final throw. Often I'd fling the rod for all I was worth only to be pinching the line against the cork. Slowly the casts got longer and straighter; gradually, almost imperceptibly, the drifts got better.

I had what you'd call total beginner's luck that evening: I hooked a steelhead (and this in a place where, in the last two years of intense angling effort, I'd seen exactly one other steelhead caught).

Every cast before that had strung out lifeless. This one didn't. There was nothing and then all of the sudden there were the pit-bull tugs of a fish. For a second I thought I'd snagged a rock or a strong play in the current—something to make the illusion real—but then the steelhead jumped as though angled for low-orbit and I saw the orange fly pinned in the corner of his jaw and an expletive of disbelief escaped me, jumped out just like a fish. Step backward. Adjust the drag. Keep the line tight. Dear God don't let him get any slack.

After a moment the fish feels like a piece of lumber. Exhausted. Probably a buck that came in this past fall, his tanks half-empty from a winter spent beneath a yard of ice. I reach for the net on my back—*play it cool*—I fondle for it—*just wait til Andy sees this*—and in so doing I probably raised the rod tip too high or didn't pay enough attention or did any one of a million things that I'll analyze for days afterward, because in an instant the fish is wallowing ten feet from my desperate eyes and then it's not. Hook pops out. Gone. Insert expletive of a different kind as I stand there like a lost man.

When Andy hears the whole story later, he consoles me once but no more.

"*C'est la vie,*" he says.

That's another thing I like about him: he won't let you dwell on the lost fish or the what-ifs. If I mentioned the incident later, he'd ignore me. Pretty soon I realized that I ought to just shut up about it.

Now it's June. The ice on the riverbank has gone and with it the Arctic terns marauding for salmon smolt. Now it's gulls cutting the sky like the Luftwaffe; now it's a hundred people or more picketing themselves in the water, playing the lottery of salmon.

This river is one of the few that's actually open for king salmon. The rest closed down weeks ago when the fisheries managers looked at the return numbers and frowned. Blame commercial fishing, blame orcas, blame the pressure of sport anglers, blame anything. Kings are disappearing. The only reason we can fish here is because much of the early run is composed of hatchery fish. The program started in the 1970s but petered out in 2008. I once heard someone complaining about that in a fly shop in midtown Anchorage; not the fact that the hatchery closed down, but that it existed at all.

"I don't really want to fish for something out of a lab," they said. Young guy my age but with a trendy mustache. "'Specially not on my Spey rod."

Now I see him in the campground.

It's something like eight o'clock in the evening but I won't fish until ten when the sun gets low. I string up the Spey rod slowly and carefully, checking and rechecking knots because I've got the time. The fly is one of my own creations that, after three years of tinkering, is finally getting somewhere. It's got marabou and Schlappen and ostrich and rubber legs and jungle cock. Hourglass eyes and a rabbit collar. I make some percolated coffee and then it's time.

Spey fishing started popping up in North American angling literature sometime around the 1930s. It's possible—likely even—that the method was here before that, it's just that historians don't have much to go off of if it's not written down. Roderick Haig-Brown, in fact, a vaunted laureate of fly-fishing writing (actually more like a patron saint by now), drops some hints at the two-handed cast in his 1939 book, *The Western Angler*. Early mentions of the cast had little in the way of *how* to do it; just that you *should* do it.

Global goings-on came to influence Spey rod usage into the mid-1900s. Prior to the Second World War, bamboo was the dominant rod material. Heavy and fragile, these rods came to be replaced by fiberglass in the early '50s. Still, it's somewhat generous to call Spey fishing a sporting backwater in those days; few people did it and even fewer people did it well. The Space Age came and went and its effects rippled throughout technology the world over. Not only had we set foot on the Moon, launched satellites, landed probes on the surface of Mars, and lived to tell about most of it, but as of the late 1970s, a fly fisherman had cane, fiberglass, boron, and graphite to select from as their rod materials. Graphite, in particular, allowed for the creation of long rods—some up to fifteen feet—that retained their lightness and castability. Spey fishing was finally taking root in North America.

It's a couple of hours later there on the river, me hoping for a king. I've been casting long enough that it starts to feel practiced and mechanical; long enough that my shoulder is sore, anyway. My legs are numb in the water. Knees rusted. Around me the shadow world of one a.m. plays itself out. Loneliness in one direction where fishermen have vacated. Motion in the other, the low sun glinting off the hordes of sockeye fishers' tools, appearing to me like a deranged circus machine. Slashes of light. No one else fishes for kings. Odds are too low, apparently.

I'm using a Skagit shooting head and a sink-tip line. Both of these tools have undergone nearly as much advancement as the rods have. Before them, Spey casting was done with floating lines. Flies would be skated in the top tier of the water column and fish would have to come up to grab them. In a purist sense—the very same that compels anglers to fish dry flies only—this works; you're giving each fish a sporting chance, meeting them on some ethical middle ground; affording them, as Lee Wulff once said, their sanctuary of deep water. But for certain species—moody winter steelhead, say, or king salmon—floating lines make the endeavor impossible, and mark anyone employing them just a shade or two beyond insane.

Enter the early '90s, when a devoted group of steelheaders from the Pacific Northwest figured out that presenting large flies (this is where the Intruder got its start) on sink-tip lines was dastardly effective. If you're a fly angler, you know the names Ed Ward, Scott Howell, Jerry French, and their sandbox of the Skagit River; if you're not, I might as well have just told you who invented the garden hose. The problem with these sinking lines, at least at the time, was that they were long and, well, *heavy*. Existing Spey technology could not turn the lines over correctly, resulting in clunky casts and haphazard drifts. Sure, they caught the hell out of fish, but you couldn't help wondering how things could be better. That's really what Spey anglers are good at: wondering. They've usually got lots of time for it, too.

Ed Ward and his posse wondered if a short, fat line would do the trick to send all that lead-core blasting off into the airspace. Mass should theoretically equate to turn-over; more surface area connecting with the river surface gives more load to the rod, and more load to the rod gives more acceleration, more velocity, and more power to the entire system. Turns out they were right. The first Skagit head was born.

I set up another cast and release it, now toward the darkling sky. The fly leaves with the whistle of a bottlerocket, six inches from my ear. Skagit head cutting the air. I'm still rooted to the same spot. Maybe at one point I tried to count the casts but I don't anymore. Each one is new; a shuffle of the deck. The more I think about it, each one becomes a passage of decades, too, because what began as the Welsh throw and got described and replicated and honed with new technology is here now. The same monotony and the same hope. Old but new.

The whole thing's like an algorithm. You pick up a Spey rod, let's say, either out of idle curiosity at the fly shop or from the depths of a long-awaited package that's finally arrived on your doorstep in midwinter. It's clear from first glance that there's something special about the rod. Some inexplicable arithmetic taking place within the cork. There's the weight of centuries, somehow, whether or not you've read Art Lingren's book. A pedigree that even the most ignorant can't deny. At first it might seem like a decent tool for wasting some time on the river. Something to look cool with; to flash around and carry backwards and laurel yourself with. Then as you turn the rod in hand, maybe test its wiggle, the algorithm will reach its crux. You'll *have* to cast it, if only ineptly, because you'll have to feel it. And then it'll happen: you'll hook a fish or have some other seemingly improbable experience—like a steelhead at sunset, for example—and all of the casting that once seemed mildly entertaining will become a sustenance for the mind.

You'll make a flawless Snap-T, and in between the snap and the D-loop, while you're thinking about something neat like blue-winged teal or how you got all the chips in your windshield, your subconscious will tackle something else: that surface area makes load, that load makes power, that power means length and length means depth and more time in the zone compounds the low odds which you may or may not have accepted already. Law of averages. Doesn't guarantee anything but at least keeps the time from being wasted. Then you've gotta give some and take some and lose some and gain some and maybe at the end of the day or the end of the season you'll come out ahead with a fish, or maybe just a lot of casting practice like I did. Maybe you'll abandon things in the meantime. Expectation. Worry. Stuff you don't need anymore. That's the calculus of Spey.

After three days of casting I finally hook a king. Deep in the swing toward the end. It squirrels out a few feet of line and I keep my hand near the reel and just as soon as it arrived from that impossible gloom, it's gone. Andy's there again and he consoles me once but no more. Could've been wild or it could've been a hatchery fish. I'll never know. *C'est la vie.*

Ten minutes later, Andy hooks and manages to land a wild fish. Twelve pounds or so, sterling silver. What's there to do but share beers in the dark.

MORE TIME

Between the gravel popcorning up into the old truck's chassis and the shortgrass prairie unspooling either side of me, I come to a thought:

I couldn't have grown up anyplace but Wyoming.

Dad's next to me jostling us over a two-track that passes as a county road, saying nothing, saying everything. Yeah, duh—I couldn't have grown up anywhere else because I was planted in Wyoming, and to my knowledge there are no alternate dimensions where I could have grown up in, say, Ohio at the same time. What I mean is that the place shaped me. The way wind shapes limestone into towering ship keels, or the way it blows so hard and so constant that the cottonwoods grow diagonally. The thought never occurred to me while I was doing the growing-up. Stuff like that rarely does. I just did what any kid would do; I wandered aimless and took my freedom for granted and lived the good with the bad and figured it was all part of that celestial arithmetic known as fate.

The good: Crawling back under the fence after an evening of bass fishing on the river, mosquitos whining in your ears along with all the excuses you'll tell Mom for coming home late. Running wild like horses on Friday afternoons.

The bad: Driving across any decent stretch of the state, because there are arthropods that evolve faster than Wyoming passes by sometimes. So flat and empty and boring. Kill me if we have to drive so far as Lusk.

But now Dad stops the truck and I look out into the empty and the boring and think of all the stuff I missed as a kid. I had no idea sharp-tailed grouse existed back then, for example. Now I'm plugging a double gun with shells the day after Thanksgiving, hoping to flush one of these birds and shoot it. Dad's doing the same on the other side of the truck.

I suppose maybe I'm wrong. Maybe I *could've* grown up someplace else. I've been living in Alaska for nine years where the mountains and the forests are close, and that's suited me fine. Great, actually. But now the feel of grass crackling under my boots and the comforting openness of the land fills me, falls into me like cogs. My factory settings. Some people are predisposed with heart conditions or athletic ability or even just blue eyes; for me it's Wyoming.

All of this nostalgia was taking place on a long-overdue visit home. My grandfather—Mom's dad—had passed away after a miserable glide down the dementia ramp about a month before. With grief came relief. He and Grandma lived in Idaho when I was a kid and then I moved to Alaska for college, so I hadn't seen either of them in I couldn't tell you how long. I remember thinking about that the night Mom called me and said Grandpa had passed. He'd become a stranger to me, and I to him.

"Should I try and come to the funeral?" I can still taste the question.

Mom waited on the other end, thinking. There were tears in her voice before but not then.

"People spend all this money to travel to someone's funeral," she said. "If you're not going to see them when they're alive, why do it when they're not?"

I told her I loved her and we hung up.

Mom says a lot of things like that. So poignant it turns her supple voice into a pair of vice grips. I bought a plane ticket home to Wyoming a few days later. Not to see anyone when they were dead, but to give them a little more time while they were alive.

I LANDED IN DENVER AT SEVEN O'CLOCK on Thanksgiving morning. The airport was a ghost town. Dad was waiting at the baggage claim carousel somehow looking both older and the same as he ever had. Parents are like that. You know they deteriorate just like anything else—more liver spots, creakier knees—but somehow it's so natural you don't see it.

Driving home with Dad is like taking a college course in natural history, automotive mechanics, Mountain West biology, natural resources management, and land surveying. It can consist of flurries of conversation that last for entire counties, or it can be total silence measured on the order of hours. Dad is a major fan of backroads—*the* major fan of backroads, I should say—so our route usually involves a lot of gravel, a confusing series of turns that no one but Dad can remember, and a procession of quaint little farm towns, each with at least one abandoned grain silo and a pleasingly simple name like Hereford or Grover. I can't prove it, but I believe Dad's ultimate ambition is to make it from Denver to our family farm in southeastern Wyoming without seeing more than ten other vehicles. Along with nursing an affinity for these quiet thoroughfares, Dad's the ultimate people-hater. He's got high-blood pressure and I suspect the only reason is that people outside his immediate family exist. You should see him at baseball games.

Anyway, he's spent years refining his route to achieve near-total solitude. He used to travel a lot for work and could practice new alternatives pretty much on the weekly. I don't know if it was because of the holiday, or if he had finally reached some impossibly neglected arrangement of county roads and state highways, but on Thanksgiving we barely saw anyone. Colorado turned into Wyoming.

In his book *The Lost Continent*, Bill Bryson writes, "You can't beat the phone company, you can't make a waiter see you until he's ready to see you, and you can't go home again."

I've slowly learned this truth to be irrefutable. Never mind the phone company and the waiter; not going home again is a tough one. It's especially tough as we turn onto the dirt tract that'll take you past the Frasers' and then the Buschs' and finally to Mom and Dad's mailbox.

Home hasn't changed. It's still the same blue sky that can turn to sideways blizzard at the drop of a hat, the same thirsty cottonwoods grasping at the clouds, the same yellow dogs that come spilling out the screen door as soon as Dad stops the truck.

Okay, maybe home *has* changed. Dogs show this most of all, the old ones especially. Doc is that old one, a wizened Lab hobbling across the pavement to say hello like he just saw me yesterday. We got him when I was a sophomore in high school. My brother Hank left a few years after that for college, so Doc became my brother. We'd lay by the woodstove for hours, his ribcage my pillow as I'd try to do homework. He'd ride shotgun through the early mornings of checking traps before school. Now time shows itself in his bleaching fur and in the fatty tumors that lump themselves onto his body. The dog that once leaped onto the four-wheeler to go gopher trapping can now barely get up the porch steps. These days, with the time that passes between my visits, I'm not sure which goodbye with Doc will be the last one.

Pete, on the other hand, shows that home has changed in his very existence. Mom and Dad got him about two years ago, well after I'd left the house. He comes from a line of pedigreed pointing Labs in northeastern Colorado and is the canine equivalent of a Jet-Ski.

I'd been telling Dad for weeks that I was going to take Pete hunting every day that I could while I was there. I'd turned head-over-heels for the whole upland hunting thing during the previous year, and being home provided the opportunity to chase new species in new places—or at least new species in familiar places. It was also a rare chance to hunt in November, when Alaska is normally covered over in three feet of snow and the grouse have all but disappeared into it. Dad was up for it; I figured Pete would be, too.

So there we were the next morning, wandering the sharptail country, Pete casting huge circles in front of us, peeing on cow pies and pointing sticks. I'm not kidding. He points sticks. Dad was carrying a beast of a twelve-gauge made by SKB back in the '80s; thick old double barrels, a slickened glossy stock, beavertail forend. I was toting a relic of Dad's, as well: an SKB twenty-gauge that looked as snappy as it felt.

Maybe it's the newness of this whole upland pursuit, but carrying a double-gun just makes me feel special. Childlike. I'm not sure why that can be, because I don't associate my childhood with bird guns or even bird hunting at all. I can count the bird hunts I went on with one hand. I'll tell you about a few of them later, maybe. Perhaps what I'm feeling is the fascination of something new. Following Pete through ocean-big prairie, watching Dad way off to the right and knowing somehow he's enjoying himself. I could be wrong about all of that, too, I guess.

We stop to marvel at an ancient stock tank and a rancher's handiwork there. Whoever it was built a big rain catcher out of sheet tin, inclining it just so to let the rain dribble into a home-made gutter and into the tank. It was built years ago; possibly more than I'd seen in my life. The section of pasture had since become a walk-in public hunting ground, and for all I know the rancher is dead.

DAD DOESN'T SAY MUCH AS WE HEAD OUT to go hunting the next day. To be fair, he rarely says much, and if he does it's usually about who owns what patch of land or some farm project he's wanting to finish. That's how it was when I was a kid. Long spells of silence. They'd turn into droughts that I'd try to fill with questions or dumb observations.

"How does a flywheel work?"

"I bet bobcats would like that tangly country up there."

These days the questions and observations are blander, more mundane. I've grown up a little and much of what was unknown and deliciously mysterious back then is now grasped. I know how flywheels work, for example. What I don't know is how people afford houses, or how they raise children.

We're headed out for sharptails again, this time in a more promising location where Ryan Kelly, who was also visiting home, said he'd seen a flock not two days before. We'd risen in the dark to coffee and tittering dog claws. The next four mornings, it would turn out, would be just like that. Rocking around on corrugated two-tracks, Pete whining from the backseat. Dad broke the silence that second morning by suggesting we walk the cornfield edge first, then hunt the shortgrass on the other side of the road. Sounded good to me.

The November sun spilled over the horizon. You hear about sharptails being the proverbial needle in a haystack, but that doesn't really resonate until you're in their world, looking out upon miles and miles of likely country, boots stoic like they know they'll have to walk it all. A big anvil of those words once conjured—*desolate, empty, boring*—closes in like a thunderhead, but now they're pleasing, welcomed like old friends.

There's no edge habitat to direct our route. There's only grass about calf-high and the slight folding of hills. Way off in the distance I can see a sickle of rocks that Dad and I once clambered up when I was twelve years old, looking for antelope. Among the many things I didn't know, apparently I didn't know the buck from the doe in the herd we found and I blasted a .270 round in her direction. It was just as well because my scope was off and the bullet passed harmlessly between her ears.

We bump a jackrabbit about a mile on. My knuckles tighten on the gun but I don't draw. Off he goes like an asteroid. Pete is oblivious and remains that way. The dog's got some things to learn.

What's peculiar about hunting is that it doesn't totally wipe away other thoughts. I'm still thinking about the 'what-ifs' as Dad and I trudge the country—what if Emmie and I bought a house, what if we have a child, what if my teaching job gets ripped out from under me, that sort of thing. Questions without easy answers but usually associated with enough money to fund an island nation's revolution. I'm not thinking about them directly, but I'm not totally oblivious to them, either. It's more like the gun in my hand is a mental snake catcher; holding the actual thought at arm's length so I can chew on it more comfortably. Eyes peeled for sharptails, mind running numbers in the background. Pretty soon we're a hundred yards from the truck and it happens. Sharptails get up wild, six of them, laughing at our buffoonery, flying big over the horizon to Canada for all I know.

A seedling of shame takes root in my gut. It grows. I could've shot. They weren't that far and the gun's choked modified and full. So why didn't I. Why didn't I. *You miss a hundred percent of the shots you don't take, Mr. Gretzky.*

You forget all about houses and kids at a time like that.

NEXT DAY, WE HUNT A PATCH OF PUBLIC LAND over by the Nebraska border. Along with everyone else and their brother, it turns out. It had snowed a bit the night before and we got there early. Pre-dawn early, when the dark was still king and you could barely make out the ghostly shapes of trees. We sat there quietly for several moments, until finally it was light enough to see and, according to the clock, to legally shoot at something.

We hunted strips of juniper trees first. That's about as far as my pheasant instinct could take me. Like I said, I didn't grow up hunting birds, so I felt like someone trying out ice skating for the first time. I'd done it alone for the last several years, sure, but it wasn't in this type of landscape, and it wasn't with Dad.

I wonder—again—if he's enjoying himself. I wonder if he knows that I'm over here just trying to take back a childhood where I wished I'd spent more time hunting with him, because now I'm on the downhill of my twenties and he's almost sixty-three. That's still plenty of time, you could say, and maybe I'm telling myself the same thing somewhere in my subconscious. But what surfaces most often is that I wish it was more. More time to hunt, more silence in the truck, more backroads between here and Denver.

It's not long before we hear the first shots of our competitors. We come over a little rise and there's a string of blaze orange way out ahead. I hear the sharp echoing directive of one of the men—*Dead bird!*—and the white blur of a setter flits through the grass.

That's what a lot of hunters live for. Pheasant hunting for pen-raised birds. In a way I pity them; I'd rather hunt wild sharptails, wild anything, really, and get nothing at all than slay a limit of roosters that were picking grit out of a net pen two days ago. It's easy to get snobbish like that when *you* haven't shot anything. Then Dad spots a fresh bird track and follows it maybe ten feet and whispers, "*There he is!*" and I forget all about pen-raised versus wild when I see the rooster's proud silhouette strutting down the two-track.

I take Pete and we make chase, the pheasant instantly guessing our intentions and legging it like an Olympic sprinter.

He burst from the ground with a fury that you'd expect from a creature with a keeled breastbone, and even though you hope for it, hunt all day for it, it still scares the bejesus out of you when it happens. I blasted off a shot in the pandemonium, knocking some tail feathers loose but otherwise leaving the rooster unharmed. We hunted some tree rows carefully after that, trying to find him, but we never did. Most of the birds had dipped across the fence to private ground.

We took a roundabout walk back to the truck. I think we talked about houses and property and investments along the way. Maybe children, too. I made like I understood the subjects, casual as I could, but when it came right down to it I spoke what I felt.

"It scares me."

At first I wasn't sure Dad had heard me, because he knelt down and started looking at coyote tracks. They were all over the place. Had to be a bumper crop of the things. After a while he got back up.

"It's a big decision."

Back in the truck, the popcorn of gravel, Dad takes the curves hard out toward a reservoir where we watch the geese pile on and off like starlings.

"It sure scares me," I said again. To fill the silence, I don't know. I figured Dad wouldn't say anything else, but he did.

"That's because it *is* scary," he said. "But that's what you're supposed to do. You grow up."

PETE AND I SLEPT LIKE TREES THAT NIGHT. The forecast in the morning showed a storm moving in late that afternoon, so we made quick plans to sneak out for a last-ditch sharptail hunt. Dad didn't go; the past three days of tromping around—or was it four?—had his knees in bad shape, so he hung around the house and did a few of his farm chores.

It was a morning like any other. Wind rattling against the side of the truck as we drove south. Houses and kids and grandparents and life and death swimming behind the only real thought I could put my finger on:

God, let there be birds.

Turns out He acquiesced to that request: a rabble of pheasants wandered like gypsies about fifty yards from the truck right as I parked. I loaded the gun and let Pete out and off the birds went. One rooster remained footbound so I chased him until he flushed; then I gave him one barrel of the ol' twenty-gauge, then another, and he thunked to the ground. You couldn't write it or paint it better; the western horizon blew up in the kinds of colors that cameras don't capture. Your mind doesn't even capture them quite right.

So we had a bird. My first pheasant on the wing, actually, which is a pretty big deal. You can make the case that houses and kids and real jobs are the badges of growing up, but I'd counter with things like pheasants and deer. Dead things ask a lot of a person.

My first dead pheasant happened when I was eight. We were hunting with my uncle and cousin down by Hawk Springs and Dad spotted a rooster frozen mid-stride through the grass. He put the twelve-gauge in my hands, helped me steady it, and I killed the bird. Hey-alright. I hunted pheasants only one other time with Dad growing up. We tromped through the weeds where the hay mower couldn't reach up behind the house, and right in the thick of the cover a pheasant whirred up and I didn't even shoot.

"That was your chance," Dad had said.

Now I'd had a chance and I'd taken it. I held the rooster in my hands and Pete licked the feathers and I put the bird in my game vest and carried it around the rest of the day as we hit up the sharp-tail pastures.

The first pasture was empty. The second one wasn't. It was a patch of walk-in ground across from a farm where about a dozen or so birds mucked around until they flew off into the prairie. I hopped the fence and Pete slithered underneath and off we went. The covey busted up far out ahead, giggling like thieves. Over the next hill that Pete and I kept our eyes glued to.

We get there and off they go again. Birds boiling up from the shortgrass. Mottled specters the color of Wyoming.

The first shot folds one. I say that passively because I don't remember mounting the gun or pulling the trigger or the other shot that I took and missed. I remember only the instant before the bird fell; the periwinkle sky streaked with mare's tail clouds, the throttling wings of a creature beating against the wind, a bird that brought me home again.

Maybe all the hunting the last few days had been my way of making up for things. Buying more time hunting with Dad because I'd squandered so many years of it before. *Carpe diem.* But in that moment I realized that I didn't have to hold onto what was before, because it was still there. How the land was is how the land will stay. Pastures and sharptails. Hold onto now and just guess where the birds will be, where they'll get up next. I can't have a childhood of hunting with Dad back but who says I can't make a new one. Hunting and fishing and all of it are just a bunch of returns to naivety and innocence, a process of surrendering to the whims of something beyond you. Recollections and echoes and scars, sometimes.

I think back to the morning Dad and I hunted those pen-raised pheasants with everyone else and their brother. The tailfeathers I knocked loose.

It all felt right, somehow. Following Dad through the snow, him pointing out bird tracks, then the bird. Me missing two shots. Both of us grumbling about all the people and heading back to the truck, saying lots and saying little. But what felt the most right, the most like Dad and the most like what I grew up with, was sitting and waiting in the truck before first light. There was absolutely nothing exceptional about it. Nothing profound that Dad said. No epiphany that sparked and caught in my brain.

I may have thought about my grandfather, and I might not have.

I may have thought of ways to prove Bill Bryson wrong, or maybe not.

In the actual play of the world, we only sat waiting for maybe four minutes. Pete was too amped and Dad and I were watching the road for other headlights. But now, here in the words as I write them, those four minutes in the dark just before legal shooting light can last forever. Dad's knees don't wear out and Pete and Doc live forever and I don't have to wish for more time. The stories can linger and replay and spin themselves together like those yarns Dad and Jim and Ted used to tell. It's a cycle as old as time, as old as the sun: you've got the passion to chase the dark, chase it right off the horizon, and somewhere in between all those early mornings you grow up and look back occasionally, and that's what you're supposed to do.

Maybe I'm wrong, but I doubt it.

"Fiberglass Daydream" is a truncated version of a story by the same name which appeared in The Flyfish Journal, Volume 13.4

"The Shape of Hares" first appeared in the Winter 2022 issue of Strung Sporting Journal

"Chasing the Dark" contains pieces of a story known as "The Situk Tales," originally published in the Oct/Nov 2022 issue of Fly Fisherman Magazine.

"Pluto & Ptarmigan" first appeared in the Winter 2023 issue of Strung Sporting Journal

"More Time" contains pieces of a story known as "Boring," originally published in the 2023 Bird Hunting Edition of Gray's Sporting Journal

NOTES

Most of the thoughts in this book are my own and most of the information is anecdotal. That's how it goes with hunting and fishing. However, there were certain cases where further research of other sources was warranted to more completely reflect on my experiences. In these cases, my research trails are documented below. Chase the dark, sure, but don't forget to chase knowledge every now and then, too.

-JJ

God Save the Whitefish:

Regarding rocks: If you have even a passing interest in Alaskan geology, a copy of Cathy Connor and Daniel O'Haire's *Roadside Geology of Alaska* (Mountain Press, 1988) is a must-have. It's fun to know about the rocks in this great state as you drive past them. It's also fun to think about how puny you are in the scheme of things.

Fossils & The Fourth of July:

Regarding "Lizzie" the Hadrosaur: I am a fully-fledged dinosaur nerd, and as such, any and all newsworthy dinosaur discoveries in Alaska are logged in my brain as 'majorly important.' Such is the case with "Lizzie" the hadrosaur and the gravel quarry where she was found. I read once, long ago—probably on a Wikipedia page—that a hadrosaur had been found in the Matanuska Formation near the Glenn Highway, but it wasn't until I found Anne D. Pasch's and Kevin C. May's 1997 research article on the find that I obtained specifics. Titled "First Occurrence of a Hadrosaur (Dinosauria) From The Matanuska Formation (Turonian) in The Talkeetna Mountains of South-central Alaska," this paleontologically-titillating piece was published in the Alaska Division of Geological & Geophysical Surveys series, *Short Notes on Alaska Geology*. Check it out. And stop to appreciate Lizzie's quarry sometime.

Pluto & Ptarmigan

Regarding Pluto: Pluto is an endlessly fascinating subject—both the planet itself and its humble discovery—and I was satiated by a number of resources. Primary among these was Alan Stern and David Grinspoon's exhaustively-detailed and thrilling account of the first Pluto mission called *Chasing New Horizons* (Picador, 2018). Additionally, the Lowell Observatory in Flagstaff, Arizona (from which Pluto was first definitively observed almost a century ago) maintains an excellent website. Madison Mooney's 2021 blog post there—"Who Was Clyde Tombaugh?"—is an intriguing history of the Kansas farm boy's monumental discovery (https://lowell.edu/who-was-clyde-tombaugh/).

Regarding Ptarmigan: I'm a dinosaur nerd, I'm a space nerd, and I'm an etymology nerd. I like knowing how things got their names. The story of the word *ptarmigan* is an altogether fascinating one, and its varied pieces are assembled neatly in a 2021 blog post by author and etymologist Paul Anthony Jones (https://www.haggardhawks.com/post/ptarmigan).

The Calculus of Spey

Regarding Spey History: If you want a rigorously-researched compendium of Spey history, look no further than Art Lingren's 2006 *The Spey Cast or Welsh Throw: History in Great Britain, Roots in British Columbia and Popularity in North America*. That's what I did, anyway. These days, as I attempt to wrestle my own Spey rod and the results come out looking like a kindergartner's joyride, I can at least think about what a wonderful history the tool in my hand has.

Regarding Fly Histories: One of my big-ish writing projects in 2021 was a series of fly tyer profiles for the *Fish Alaska Magazine* website. My goal was to seek out the origins of Alaska's most famous flies and tell the stories of their creators. It was through these efforts that I met some of the craft's very best. Most of the history in this chapter regarding Ed Ward, his Intruder fly, and Skagit heads came from an interview with George Cook (creator of the Alaskan Popsicle fly and notable Spey king salmon pioneer) in 2021. You can check it out at https://www.fishalaskamagazine.com/george-cook-the-legend/.

Photo by Emelia Jackson

JOSEPH JACKSON IS A SOCIAL STUDIES TEACHER and outdoor writer in Alaska. His work has appeared in many publications such as *Gray's Sporting Journal, Fly Fisherman, The Drake, Alaska Magazine*, and others, where his wife, Emmie, also publishes much of her photography. His first book, *It's Only Fishing*, has garnered immense praise throughout the outdoor world. When he's not getting up early to chase rainbow trout or hunt ptarmigan, he's learning how to be a father to the world's next greatest fly-fisherwoman. You can reach out to him at josephdjacksonwriter.com.

www.ingramcontent.com/pod-product-compliance
Lightning Source LLC
Chambersburg PA
CBHW011550070526
44585CB00023B/2530